IMAGES
of America

CHILDREN'S MEMORIAL
HOSPITAL OF CHICAGO

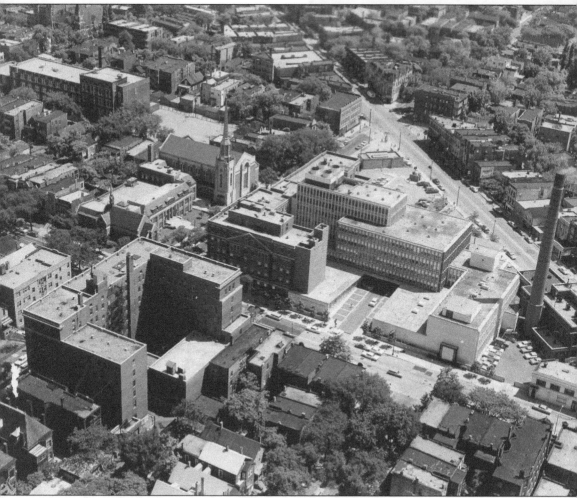

The triangle bounded by Lincoln Avenue, Fullerton Avenue, and Orchard Street served as the core of the Children's Memorial campus from 1908 and is seen in this view looking to the southeast, with Lincoln Avenue across the top right. The photograph was taken in the early 1970s, prior to the construction of the parking garage (1976), the Kroc Building (1981), and the additional floors of the bed tower (1982). Donations from grateful patient families and the larger community were instrumental in funding improvements and expansion throughout the years to advance medical care for children.

ON THE COVER: This earliest known clinical photograph from Children's Memorial Hospital dates from 1886 and depicts Truman W. Miller, MD, the hospital's first president of the medical staff, in surgery. From its humble beginning as an eight-bed unit in Lincoln Park, Children's Memorial Hospital grew to become one of America's premier children's hospitals, providing unsurpassed care to children and fulfilling founder Julia Foster Porter's mission "to provide care for children regardless of race, creed, or ability to pay."

IMAGES
of America

CHILDREN'S MEMORIAL
HOSPITAL OF CHICAGO

Stanford T. Shulman, MD

ARCADIA
PUBLISHING

Published by Arcadia Publishing
Charleston, South Carolina

Library of Congress Control Number: 2013439840

For all general information, please contact Arcadia Publishing:
Telephone 843-853-2070
Fax 843-853-0044
E-mail sales@arcadiapublishing.com
For customer service and orders:
Toll-Free 1-888-313-2665

Visit us on the Internet at www.arcadiapublishing.com

*Dedicated to my family and to the millions of patients treated
at Children's Memorial Hospital, their families, and all who
contributed to their care over 130 outstanding years*

CONTENTS

ACKNOWLEDGMENTS

The origin of this book was a 2011 request by the Medical Education Board of the Department of Pediatrics (chair, Ellen Chadwick, MD) for a special presentation regarding the 130-year history of Children's Memorial Hospital (CMH). The occasion was the impending closure of CMH and move to Ann & Robert H. Lurie Children's Hospital of Chicago in June 2012. From that seed germinated the concept of a book to memorialize CMH. All royalties from this work will accrue to the hospital. Unless otherwise specified, all images appear courtesy of the Lurie Children's archives. To attempt to encapsulate the entire history of CMH into a book of this size with its emphasis on photographs and relatively few words cannot do justice to the vast numbers of programs, areas of remarkable expertise, laypersons, volunteers, professionals, and others in the CMH community who have contributed so much to the success of the institution and to the children. I acknowledge here all those who could not be specifically cited.

Most instrumental in assisting me in putting the pieces together for this work and for providing superb editorial advice, wordsmithing, and counsel has been Vita Lerman, public affairs, who has declined the offer to be coauthor (even though she has earned it!). Special thanks are due to Patrick Magoon, longtime president and chief executive officer of Children's Memorial and now Lurie Children's, and to Founders' Board presidents Sarah Baine and Lauren Gorter for their interest and support of this project. Claire Peterson, audiovisual, provided excellent technical photographic support. Special thanks also go to librarians Carol Jeuell (at CMH) and Ron Sims (at Northwestern University Feinberg School of Medicine) for responding to my urgent requests for specific information. Others whose assistance must be acknowledged include Robert Miller; Drs. Margaret O'Flynn, Alex Muster, and Gilbert Given for their recollections; Julie Pesch and Kathleen Keenan of public affairs; the staff of Lurie Children's Foundation; and Liliana Balaguer for secretarial assistance.

A bibliography for this work includes Clare McCausland's *An Element of Love* (1981); annual reports of CMH (1906–2012); Thomas Bonner's *Medicine in Chicago 1850–1950* (1957); *History of Medicine and Surgery and Physicians and Surgeons of Chicago* (1922); Isaac Abt's *Pediatrics* (1923); *Holt's Diseases of Infancy and Childhood 10th Ed.* (1936), edited by L. Emmett Holt and Rustin McIntosh; the *Mitchell-Nelson Textbook of Pediatrics 5th Ed.* (1950), edited by Waldo E. Nelson; and Dr. Matt Steiner's lecture on the centennial of CMH in 1982.

INTRODUCTION

This book honors Chicago's Children's Memorial Hospital (CMH), which served the children of Chicago (and far beyond) for 130 years—from its founding in 1882 until June 2012, when it moved to a state-of-the-art facility. It was renamed Ann & Robert H. Lurie Children's Hospital of Chicago and moved to the campus of Northwestern University Feinberg School of Medicine (NUFSM). During its long and distinguished existence, CMH impacted a large number of Chicago metropolitan area families. We hope to capture here the spirit of those professionals and lay individuals who provided the best possible medical care to well over a million children with expertise and compassion, and recognize the essential administrative and philanthropic support.

CMH evolved from an 8-bed cottage to a 288-bed hospital, one of America's finest. Services steadily broadened with advances in medicine and the hospital became a world-class child health-care facility with internationally known physicians and surgeons. CMH was a teaching hospital for 103 years, with academic affiliations with Rush Medical College (1909–1919), University of Chicago (1919–1946), and, particularly, Northwestern University (1946–present).

The spectrum of patients at CMH changed dramatically, mirroring changes in childhood illnesses and phenomenal technologic innovations that reduced morbidity and mortality immensely. In the late 19th century, children suffered primarily from malnutrition, failure to thrive ("general debility"), and infections, particularly typhoid, tuberculosis, rheumatic fever, and rheumatic heart disease. By the early 21st century, CMH hospitalizations mainly involved organ transplantation, immunocompromised hosts, congenital defects, and various chronic diseases.

CMH owed its existence to its founder and major benefactor, the remarkable Julia Foster Porter. Grieving after elder son Maurice Foster Porter succumbed to acute rheumatic fever in 1881, Julia Porter had the vision to found Illinois's first children's hospital to provide free care to sick children. She insured its success through her meticulous management and total financial support for many years. Exclusively free care was provided until 1926, when some private and semiprivate beds were first established.

In the late 19th century, Chicago was America's fastest-growing city, with 30,000 people in 1850, 500,000 in the 1880s, and 2 million in 1910. Extensive rebuilding and expansion occurred in the decades after the 1871 Great Fire, which decimated much of the city, including the Porter home at Clark Street and Belden Avenue in Chicago's Lincoln Park. Construction was shoddy, overcrowding severe, and, in many areas, most homes lacked indoor plumbing. The meatpacking industry attracted many immigrants and other impoverished individuals, helping to create unsanitary conditions considered worse than in New York, Philadelphia, or Baltimore. Conditions were particularly dire in areas with severely crowded tenements and poor sewage systems. Infectious diseases including typhoid (5,000 cases in 1886), diarrheal disorders, tuberculosis, and smallpox were widespread. Children under five accounted for most Chicago deaths, reaching 70.7 percent in 1871, exceeding other cities. Tainted milk, food, and water all contributed to childhood mortality. Child labor was also a serious problem.

No Illinois health care facility was devoted to children before Julia Porter opened her hospital in 1882. Only Dr. Mary Thompson's Chicago Hospital for Women and Children, founded in 1865 (rebuilt after the Great Fire as the Mary Thompson Hospital) for "women and children of the respectable poor," with a capacity of 14 had a few children's beds. Chicago had no practitioners of the new specialty of pediatrics.

Julia Porter opened her eight-bed hospital (Maurice F. Porter Memorial Hospital) in a Lincoln Park building she owned (on the southeast corner of Belden Avenue and Halsted Street, later the site of CMH's Belden Building) to provide free care to children 3–13 years old irrespective of race, creed, or ability to pay. She then purchased the northwest corner of Fullerton Avenue and Orchard Street, where a 20-bed hospital opened in 1886, expanding in 1896 to 50 beds. Patient volumes grew slowly. The hospital had an all-voluntary, part-time medical staff led by surgeon Truman W. Miller, who was joined in 1891 by Walter S. Christopher (a nationally prominent pediatrician), and others. A Board of Lady Managers was appointed in 1892, with incorporation and naming of a Board of Directors in 1894.

By 1903, the need for major reorganization was clear. The hospital name was changed to Children's Memorial Hospital, the Board of Directors was reorganized, and the Lady Managers became the Auxiliary (now the Founders') Board, with new bylaws and constitution. With Julia Porter's generous financial assistance, purchase of the triangle bounded by Lincoln Avenue, Fullerton Avenue, and Orchard Street enabled expansion, under board leadership from 1904–1952 of John P. Wilson, Thomas D. Jones, and then John P. Wilson Jr., from a family facility to one with wider philanthropic support. Important construction included Maurice Porter Memorial Pavilion (1908) and Agnes Wilson Memorial Pavilion (1912) side by side on Fullerton Avenue, and the Cribside Building on Orchard Street (1908), which included infant beds. The pavilion model was thought to reduce the spread of contagious diseases. Medical leadership included Dr. Frank S. Churchill, a national pediatric leader, from 1908 until he left for World War I in 1917.

Clinical services were added as space increased, with an outpatient clinic and dispensary (1902), X-ray department (1907), and visiting nurse program (1905), which became the Social Service department (1912). In 1912, the Otho S.A. Sprague Memorial Institute supported research laboratories and a fellow, beginning a 100-year affiliation. Clinical volumes continued to grow; in 1920, CMH served 2,492 inpatients and 14,390 children, with 30,000 outpatient visits.

Philanthropic support of CMH dates from its opening and was critical. Julia Porter successfully solicited friends and associates to endow beds at $250–$500/bed annually, enabling free patient care. The Auxiliary Board opened the White Elephant Rummage Shop (1918), raising over $10 million for CMH by 2012. World War I substantially impacted staff in 1917–1919, with at least 10 physicians and 6 nurses/graduates involved. The 1918 influenza epidemic claimed 8,500 lives in Chicago from September to November 1918, including two nursing graduates.

In 1921, Dr. Joseph Brennemann became the chief of staff, serving until 1940. One of America's most respected and renowned pediatricians, he was one of the most important physician leaders responsible for CMH's steady growth. The first full-time salaried physician at CMH (1930), he oversaw substantial expansion of both physical facilities and physician staff. New clinics included orthopedics, cardiology, syphilis, diabetes, and nephritis.

The Martha Wilson Memorial Pavilion opened in 1926 with 134 beds, including 36 private beds, the first at CMH, and remained open until 2012. On the 1886 building site, the Nellie A. Black Building opened in 1932 for nurses' residence, and the Deering Building for interns in 1933—both with tunnels to the hospital. The Thomas D. Jones Memorial Building on Orchard Street opened in 1940, primarily to expand outpatient clinics.

Key medical staff additions included future chiefs of staff Drs. Stanley Gibson (1944–1948) and John Bigler (1949–1962), and future surgeon-in-chief Willis J. Potts (1945–1960). In 1931, Brennemann brought world-famous pediatrician Dr. Isaac A. Abt, Northwestern University Medical School (NUMS) chair of pediatrics (1909–1939), to conduct teaching clinics for NUMS residents and students in the CMH amphitheater and outpatient clinics.

As the Great Depression gripped the country, the number of patients seeking free care increased further. In 1927, the outpatient department and dispensary had 36,935 visits, which increased to 47,465 in 1930, and 67,393 in 1935. Under financial pressure due in part to Depression-related decline in philanthropy, CMH first received state and county funds in 1932.

During this era, a heliotherapy facility (exposure to sun and fresh air)—popular for treatment of non-pulmonary forms of tuberculosis (spinal, bone and joint, abdominal), rickets ,and perhaps psoriasis—was built on the roof of the Agnes Wilson Pavilion (1922).

Polio epidemics continued to plague Chicago; patients came to CMH in the convalescent stage for hydrotherapy to rebuild muscle strength, for physical therapy, orthopedic surgery as needed, and occasionally to use the iron lung for respiratory support. In summer 1936, Chicago experienced the largest polio epidemic since the record year, 1917, and the hydrotherapy tank obtained in the early 1930s was used almost constantly. A large measles epidemic occurred in 1937, affecting several hospital staff.

In the 1939 *CMH Annual Report*, Brennemann writes about the astonishing benefit of the recently introduced first antibiotic, sulfanilamide/sulfapyridine: "In the many years of my medical experience there has been no comparable event . . . it has come with such suddenness and such startling effect that it seems unbelievable." This therapy, often with horse or rabbit antiserum directed specifically at Group A streptococcus, hemophilus, meningococcus, or pneumococcus, dramatically reduced mortality of pneumonia, meningitis, and other infections. This and other advances contributed to the decline in mortality among hospitalized infants less than 18 months old, from 42.6 percent in 1928 to 9.4 percent in 1939.

With Brennemann's retirement as chief of staff in late 1940, a new era began. Dr. C. Anderson Aldrich was chief of staff until 1943, succeeded by Dr. Stanley Gibson (1944–1948), who was also the NUMS chair of pediatrics (1939–1948) and instrumental in establishing the long-standing formal affiliation between CMH and NUMS in 1946. With World War II's onset in late 1941, CMH experienced medical staff shortages; 33 physicians left within seven months in 1942. Blood and sera shortages, mandated window blackouts, supply rationing, and lower occupancy (48 percent in 1943) prompted increasing the upper age limit from 13 to 15 years. The resident shortage caused by the war (18 in 1940, 11 in 1944) was alleviated by Latin American physicians, rotating interns, and female residents.

The sulfa agents, and later the miracle drug penicillin, produced dramatically higher cure rates of bacterial infections and made surgery safer. Late in the war, penicillin availability was facilitated by CMH's status as an Illinois penicillin distribution site. Polio outbreaks continued, with record numbers of post-polio patients requiring respirators in 1950. Introduction of polio vaccines in the 1950s led to dramatic reduction in polio cases.

The transition from war years to peacetime was notable for more physicians and residency applicants. By 1946, residents were at prewar levels, occupancy increased to 91 percent by 1947, and research funds from the new National Institutes of Health (NIH), National Science Foundation, and foundations became available. By 1958, CMH research support reached $210,000, one-third of which came from the NIH.

Willis J. Potts (1895–1963), pioneer blue-baby surgeon for cyanotic congenital heart disease, became the first full-time surgeon-in-chief in 1945, serving until 1960. Potts received worldwide acclaim and became a highly effective fundraiser for CMH.

John Bigler (1896–1963) became CMH chief of staff and NUMS chair of pediatrics in 1949, serving until 1962. Bigler recognized the importance of research, in addition to outstanding patient care and teaching, in CMH becoming a leading children's hospital and by 1956 identified the need for a new hospital building and research institute. He hired additional full-time staff and directed the impressive construction that dramatically changed the CMH campus.

Subspecialization within pediatrics advanced steadily during this era. The staff grew from one full-time and three part-time physicians in 1943, to eleven full-time and one part-time physicians in 1958. Full-time staff contributed substantially to increased research activity at CMH.

During this time, the hospital continued to provide free care to needy patients. Through the 1950s, over 60 percent of patients received free care; this cost in 1958 exceeded $1 million, heavily subsidized by philanthropy.

In 1957, the Board of Directors and Woman's Board first considered a modern hospital building to replace the pavilion-style buildings. Although a consultant recommended moving to the NUMS campus, CMH decided to remain in Lincoln Park. The Maurice Porter and Agnes Wilson Pavilions and the open southern portion of the triangle were replaced by a driveway from Fullerton Avenue to Lincoln Avenue (Children's Plaza), bed tower and administrative area, and connected research building. Bigler and Delbert Price, the chief administrator, supervised building plans, with ground breaking in November 1960, and $5.5 million in philanthropic support.

Opening the new buildings in October 1962 marked a major transition for CMH. Research funding reached $2 million by 1967, and a Clinical Research Center was federally funded. Two endowed chairs from the Given Foundation supported Dr. Robert Lawson, chief of staff and NUMS chair of pediatrics (1961–1970), and Dr. Henry Nadler, a prominent researcher, head of genetics, and later chief of staff and pediatric chair (1970–1981). The Department of Surgery was led by Dr. Orvar Swenson (1960–1973), famous for his innovative Hirschsprung's disease surgery, and Dr. Lowell King (1974–1981). Increasing federal and state support of the medically indigent (Medicaid) transformed health care financing, with CMH serving as both a tertiary care resource and a primary care provider. Neighborhood clinics were first established in 1966.

A $50 million Centennial Fund for further expansion was established in the 1970s, and a development (fundraising) department was formalized. Important physical additions included the Lincoln Avenue garage (1976), Kroc Diagnostic and Treatment Tower (1981), and four additional bed tower floors. By 1980, annual outpatient visits reached 140,000.

Additional subspecialty divisions were established in the 1960s and 1970s, including gastroenterology, infectious diseases, intensive care, immunology, nephrology, neurology, allergy, neonatology, pulmonary, and nuclear medicine. Programs in these areas developed, with advances in care of cancer patients and premature infants, and management of cystic fibrosis and spina bifida, as well as many other illnesses. Renal transplantation was established in 1964. Full-time medical staff expanded to 115 by 1980, encompassing virtually every subspecialty. Child guidance and psychiatry under Dr. Henry Fineberg was established in 1954, evolving to become the Division of Psychiatry in Pediatrics, then the Department of Psychiatry in 1981, currently led by Dr. Mina Dulcan.

During its last 30 years in Lincoln Park, CMH matured into one of the finest children's hospitals anywhere, with outstanding administrative, physician, and research leadership, and remarkable levels of philanthropic support. Clinical programs expanded to encompass transplantation, innovative surgery, many acute and chronic diseases (cystic fibrosis, asthma, Kawasaki disease, congenital heart disease, other congenital anomalies, diabetes, immunodeficiencies, malignancies, and so forth), supported by anesthesia (chiefs Drs. Frank Seleny, Steven Hall, and Santhanam Suresh), pathology and clinical laboratories (chiefs Drs. Frank Crussi and Elizabeth Perlman), and medical imaging (chiefs Drs. Harvey White, Andrew Poznanski and James Donaldson). From the Emergency Department to the Intensive Care Units, clinical care was unsurpassed.

Research programs also thrived as CMH developed first-class laboratory facilities, backed by philanthropic and grant support and academic linkages to NUFSM. Educational programs expanded. Child advocacy at the local, state, and national levels increased. Fueling CMH's success was unprecedented community financial support, including the $137.5 million Hand in Hand campaign (1995–2000) and the $675 million Heroes for Life campaign (2004–2012) for Ann & Robert H. Lurie Children's Hospital of Chicago. More than 250,000 donors participated in the latter campaign, including the largest donation to any children's hospital at that time, $100 million from philanthropist Ann Lurie.

On June 9, 2012, the last child was admitted to CMH, to the infectious diseases service (at 4:00 a.m., with a neck infection) and the last patient was evaluated in the Emergency Department (at 6:35 p.m., with trisomy 21 and possible pacemaker malfunction). On that day, all 126 inpatients (plus an Emergency Department patient), some critically ill, were transported safely to Lurie Children's, 3.1 miles away, by a small army of ambulances. The doors of Children's Memorial Hospital in Lincoln Park were locked for the last time, but its impact upon the health of children in Chicago and throughout the world will always be felt.

One

THE EARLY YEARS
1882–1903

Julia Foster Porter founded the Maurice F. Porter Memorial Hospital in 1882 after her son's death and personally underwrote hospital expenses (approximately $2,000 per year) for many years.

Over its first nine years, 232 patients were admitted, peaking at 68 in 1890. Surgical cases included amputations, thoracenteses, tendon surgeries, Pott's disease (vertebral tuberculosis), tuberculous and non-tuberculous osteomyelitis, and bladder extrophy. Medical diagnoses included anemia, lobar pneumonia, "general debility," acute rheumatic fever, scarlet fever, rheumatic heart disease, tuberculosis, and typhoid fever. By 1891, the all-voluntary medical staff included two surgeons, an oculist/aurist, and three attending physicians. Hospital admissions steadily increased to 302 in 1903.

Until 1892, the hospital was directed by Julia Porter, who hired a matron (at $30/month) and two assistants (at $18/month). In 1892, Mrs. Porter organized a nine-member Board of Lady Managers, with herself as president, to manage day-to-day activities. This was later renamed the Auxiliary Board, then the Woman's Board, and finally the Founders' Board. On March 27, 1894, the hospital was incorporated with a nine-member Board of Directors, including three women, in part to facilitate acceptance of bequests. By late 1894, a constitution and bylaws were drafted by the Lady Managers and approved.

The hospital expanded to 50 beds in 1896, including an isolation ward, and pioneer pediatrician Dr. Walter Christopher strongly but unsuccessfully urged expansion to 100 beds, opening the hospital to more physicians and to medical students, and establishing an infant ward.

In 1899, the hospital name was changed to the Maurice Porter Children's Hospital, and Julia Porter deeded the building and land to the Board of Directors, but continued to pay annual operating expenses. By 1900, her poor health and staff president Miller's sudden death were challenges, but by 1902, the medical staff had increased to 16, and a building fund was established with a goal of $50,000 and 10 endowed beds. John P. Wilson, board chairman, committed to raise $20,000 for a building for contagious diseases. Holabird and Roche provided free architectural plans and Julia Porter donated $75,000 for a new fireproof building to accommodate 75 patients.

From 1882–1903, about 2,100 children were admitted, the medical staff grew from 2 to 18, and free care for all children was provided.

Hospital founder Julia Foster Porter (1846–1936) moved to the Lincoln Park neighborhood (at Clark Street and Belden Avenue) at 13. Her father, Dr. John Foster, originally from New Hampshire, had moved to Chicago in 1835 to manage his brother's estate consisting of much of Chicago's original area. In 1840, he married Nancy Smith; Julia was their third child. In 1866, Julia married Rev. Edward Porter, and in 1867, the family moved to Racine, Wisconsin, where their two sons were born. In 1874, Julia's father died of a freak head injury in a carriage accident, then Reverend Porter died of appendicitis at 36 in 1876. Julia returned to Lincoln Park in 1876 to live with her mother, but tragedy continued, and in 1881, her 13-year-old son Maurice died. The portrait below shows her as a young woman, while the Paul Frebelcock painting at left shows her at 80.

[Physician's Certificate of Death form for Maurice Foster Porter, State of Illinois, Cook County, City Board of Health]

The death certificate of Julia Porter's son Maurice, who died at age 13 on March 26, 1881, after a four-month illness, was signed by Dr. Truman W. Miller. The cause of death was "Acute Rheumatism" (acute rheumatic fever), complicated by "valvular disease of the heart (Mitral)." Acute rheumatic fever, now rare in the United States, was extremely common in the 19th century, affecting children of all social classes and commonly leading to heart disease.

Julia Porter appointed Dr. Miller (1840–1900) as president of the medical staff; he served until his death in 1900. He had cared for her father and son Maurice in their last illnesses. After his Union army service, Miller was on staff at several Chicago hospitals and the Chicago Board of Health, and founded the Chicago Polyclinic, the first medical postgraduate center in the Midwest. He was vice president of the American Medical Association Board of Trustees and interim editor of its journal.

In May 1882, Julia Porter opened the Maurice F. Porter Memorial Hospital near her home in a small three-story frame house at Belden Avenue and Halsted Street that she had inherited. At a cost of $13,000, she remodeled it to have eight beds and began to plan a larger facility. No picture of that original building exists. In 1883, she purchased land a few blocks away at the northwest corner of Orchard Street and Fullerton Avenue (later the site of the Nellie A. Black Building) for $7,980 and in 1884, she began construction on the larger building shown here, which opened in 1886 with 20 beds. The hospital's original intent was to provide exclusively free care for children 3–13 years old "without restriction as to race, color, creed or ability to pay." The hospital was staffed by volunteer doctors and professional nurses under the direction of a matron. Hospital capacity increased to 50 beds in 1896, when Julia Porter funded a $6,000 addition to the building.

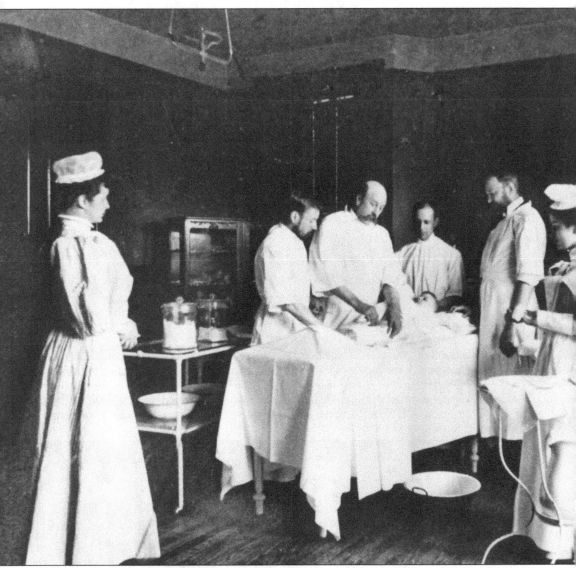

Dr. Truman W. Miller is shown in his surgery at the Maurice F. Porter Memorial Hospital in 1886, where he appears to be changing a cast or dressing a wound involving a child's left leg. This is the earliest photograph of medical care at the hospital. By 1882, antisepsis with chemicals such as carbolic acid or ethanol had recently become routine at most Chicago hospitals. However, disinfection of surgical instruments and use of gloves (asepsis) was not routine in Chicago until the 1890s. The operating room was on the hospital's top floor, the best-lit area in the 1886 building before electricity. This scene appears to be lit by daylight entering from the right. Miller (1840–1900) was the first president of the medical staff and chief surgeon at the hospital, chosen by his friend and neighbor Julia F. Porter. In 1894, Miller renovated the operating room at his own expense, providing two surgical sterilizers, a new operating table, instrument stands, and other items.

This plaque was part of the facade of the 1886 structure that was the sole building for inpatients until 1908. Construction began on this building in 1884. After demolition of the building in 1931, the plaque was stored. Around 1985, the plaque was incorporated into the sidewalk in front of the Nellie A. Black Building, erected on the same site. Because of cracking, it was removed from the sidewalk around 1995.

This rare photograph shows the sunporch of the 1886 building on Fullerton Avenue and Orchard Street around 1900, with seven children and two nurses using its space. By 1900, northern Illinois had been free of malaria for 10 years, 7 years had elapsed since the last smallpox epidemic, typhoid fever incidence was decreasing, and child labor in Chicago had declined from 9,000 in 1884 to 2,000 in 1893.

These photographs from approximately 1890 show two wards in the 1886 building, with nurses. Approximately 22 ethnically diverse patients can be seen, suggesting nearly full capacity. The light fixtures seen are a mix of gas lamps and early electric lights. The hospital was completely electrified in 1898. Julia Porter carefully reviewed and controlled all expenses as a very hands-on supervisor. She encouraged her friends and colleagues who were financially secure to benefit the hospital by endowing a bed for $250 a year to assist hospital finances. In that era, the hospital could offer a clean environment, close supervision, a nutritious diet, and a safe supply of water, milk, and food. Very few effective medications existed. Sick children from wealthier families typically received medical care at home. In 1901, after her mother's death, Julia Porter moved to Hubbard Woods (Winnetka) and became less actively involved with the hospital.

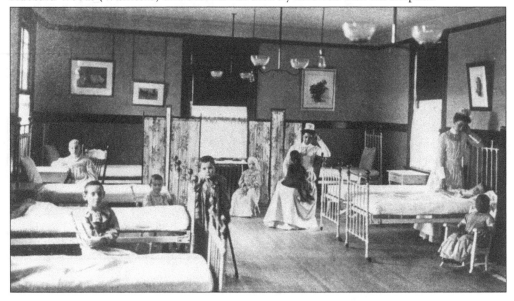

Dr. Walter Shield Christopher (1859–1905), an 1881 graduate of the Medical College of Ohio, moved to Chicago in 1890. He was a very active pediatrician at Maurice F. Porter Memorial Hospital from 1891 until his early death at age 46 in 1905, and served as president of the hospital's medical staff (1901). Christopher was a nationally prominent pioneer in child development, nutrition, and preventive pediatrics. He was elected chair of the American Medical Association's Section on Pediatrics in 1894 and vice president (1896) and president (1901–1902) of the American Pediatric Society. In his 1894 address to the AMA (shown in the photograph below), he clearly articulates the case for the separate medical specialty of pediatrics. Christopher strongly but unsuccessfully advocated lowering admission age to allow infants under 3 years old, admitting children with diarrhea with appropriate isolation precautions, and expanding the hospital to at least 100 beds.

THE
JOSEPH BRENNEMANN
LIBRARY

PEDIATRICS AS A SPECIALTY.

CHAIRMAN'S ADDRESS.

Read in the Section on Diseases of Children, at the Forty-fifth Annual Meeting of the American Medical Association, held at San Francisco, June 5-8, 1894.

BY W. S. CHRISTOPHER, M.D.
PROFESSOR OF DISEASES OF CHILDREN CHICAGO POLICLINIC; PROFESSOR OF PEDIATRICS COLLEGE OF PHYSICIANS AND SURGEONS, CHICAGO.

REPRINTED FROM
THE JOURNAL OF THE AMERICAN MEDICAL ASSOCIATION,
NOVEMBER 17, 1894.

CHICAGO:
AMERICAN MEDICAL ASSOCIATION PRESS.
1894.

Two

DEVELOPMENT OF THE TRIANGLE
1904–1920

The hospital underwent major reorganization in 1903–1904, opening a new era of expansion essential to the its future. Julia Porter approved changing the hospital's name from the Maurice Porter Children's Hospital to the Children's Memorial Hospital in 1904 to broaden its appeal. John P. Wilson served as president of the Board of Directors from 1904 to 1913 and was succeeded by Thomas D. Jones. Notably, in 1904 the mostly undeveloped four-acre triangle bordered by Fullerton Avenue, Lincoln Avenue, and Orchard Street immediately south of the 1886 building was purchased for $80,000 for further expansion, including a building on Orchard Street (Dow House). Linked to this, the hospital board received $75,000 from Julia Porter to build the Maurice Porter Memorial Pavilion to house 75 beds, which opened in 1908. The Cribside Pavilion also opened in 1908 on Orchard Street with 22 infant beds, a sunporch, and a basement milk laboratory, increasing capacity to 108 beds. Its $26,000 cost was raised by the Cribside Committee, a group comprised of young society women.

The outpatient department was first established in 1902, moved in 1905 to the Dow House, then moved in 1908 to the basement of the 1886 building, later moving again to the new Agnes Wilson Pavilion in 1913 because of steadily increasing patient volumes. X-ray equipment, a gift of Mrs. John Borland, president of the Auxiliary Board, was installed in 1907 in the 1886 building basement near the surgical wards. A series of nurses were responsible for both taking X-rays (214 X-rays in 1912) and serving as nurse-anesthetists in the early decades. In 1905, a Visiting Nurse Program was established with a part-time nurse (full-time by 1911) to investigate conditions in the home to help reduce readmissions (also a current hospital goal), evolving into the Social Service Department in 1912. A kindergarten teacher was hired in 1911, supported by Augusta Nusbaum Rosenwald, whose husband was president of Sears at the time.

The major physician leader of this era was Dr. Frank Spooner Churchill (1864–1946), a national leader in pediatrics. All physicians were voluntary until 1930, although a part-time salaried pathologist supervised the laboratories. During this era, there were two–four residents per year, the vast majority being male.

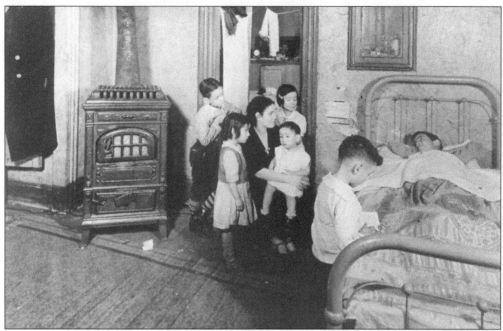

These photographs, taken by a visiting nurse, highlight the dire living circumstances of some Children's Memorial patients during the first decades after the hospital's 1882 founding. Each shows a mother with many children in an exceptionally crowded and congested living area. In the late 19th and early 20th centuries, Chicago was the fastest-growing city in America, with little indoor plumbing and high infant and child mortality rates. Safe water and milk were hard to come by and epidemics of typhoid, cholera, and other infections were common. The hospital established a Visiting Nurse Program in 1905, supported by the Board of Lady Managers and the Cribside Society. This program evolved into the Social Service Department in 1912, and by 1913, more than 3,000 home visits were made annually.

The Bambino was placed above the entrance to the Cribside Pavilion at its opening in June 1908 on Orchard Street and was officially adopted as the hospital's symbol by the Auxiliary Board in 1922. Created between 1463 and 1466 by the Florentine Italian Renaissance sculptor Andrea della Robbia for Brunelleschi's Ospedale degli Innocenti (Hospital of the Innocents) in Florence, Italy, the work contained 10 slightly different glazed terra-cotta reliefs of swaddled babies (Bambini) that still adorn the foundling hospital's loggia in Florence. This facility provided care for infants and children for more than five centuries until 1875. At Children's Memorial, the Bambino was displayed at several locations within the hospital buildings. From 1922 to 1924, several international Save the Children organizations also adopted a Bambino insignia. Shortly after its founding in 1931, the American Academy of Pediatrics also adopted the Bambino as its symbol, although details of how that occurred are unclear, and it was modified to a plumper version in 1941.

The Cribside Pavilion (shown above) opened after $26,000 for its construction was raised by the Cribside Society, a group of young society women who founded the organization in 1904. It increased hospital capacity to 108 beds, provided cribs for 22 children under three years of age, and also had a well-equipped basement milk laboratory, sunporch (photograph below), and an area for maternal instruction in care and feeding of babies. The Bambino sculpture is visible above the entrance to the Cribside Building. The Cribside Society also provided $1,500 per year for maintenance of Cribside, funding of a kindergarten teacher, individual crib endowments, and the Visiting Nurses Program. The Cribside Society evolved into the Junior Auxiliary in 1911. The photograph of the interior view of the Cribside sunporch with open windows shows the view onto the parklike grassy triangle of the campus.

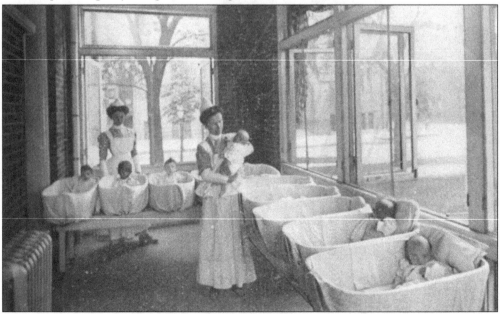

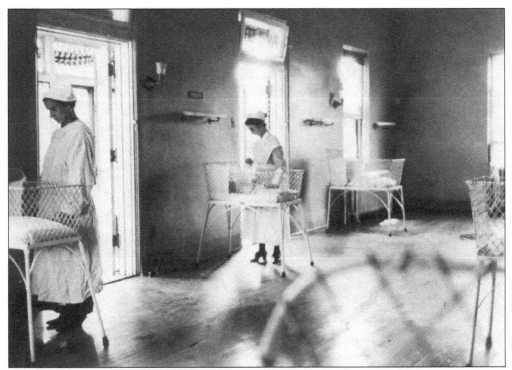

Interior views of the Cribside Pavilion from about 1910 show infants in cribs tended by nursing staff and interns in the upper-floor wards. For its day, the spacing of cribs some distance apart to reduce cross-infection is excellent, although sinks are not apparent. After a visit, Dr. Thomas Morgan Rotch of Boston, one of America's leading pediatricians, was quoted as saying that Cribside was the best-equipped infant facility in the country. Cribside was torn down in 1938 to make room for construction of the Thomas D. Jones Memorial Building; a new Cribside Building was erected in 1939 on the triangle fronting Lincoln Avenue, including a new milk laboratory.

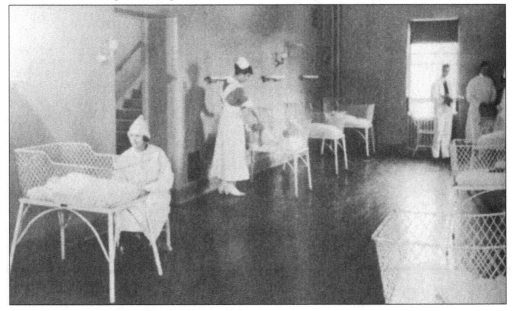

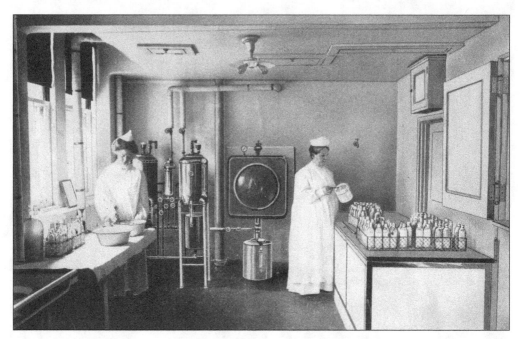

This milk laboratory in the basement of Cribside enabled a safe and steady supply for patients; it was equipped with steam sterilizers and was the only such laboratory in Chicago. The provision of safe milk for infants was critically important in this era, when commercial milk was very often adulterated and unsafe because many cows were fed only distiller's mash, were housed in filthy conditions, and some suffered with bovine tuberculosis. Consequently, the mortality rate of non-breast-fed infants was quite high, especially during summer, when it was very difficult to keep milk cold. The Chicago Milk Commission established in 1903 could not provide sufficient safe milk for the city. A replica of the CMH milk laboratory was displayed at the 1911 Child Welfare Exhibit at the Chicago Coliseum, an event headed by social worker Jane Addams.

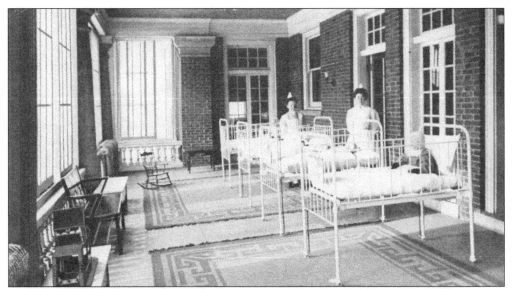

This 1909 photograph shows the pneumonia ward in the Maurice Porter Memorial Pavilion, which opened in 1908. Note how the child in the right foreground is heavily bundled, as it was thought that exposure to cold air was beneficial. Pneumonia carried a substantial mortality rate in this era, with few therapies that were beneficial. Even though anti-meningococcal antiserum was reasonably effective, antipneumococcal, antistreptococcal, or anti-hemophilus sera alone were not very effective.

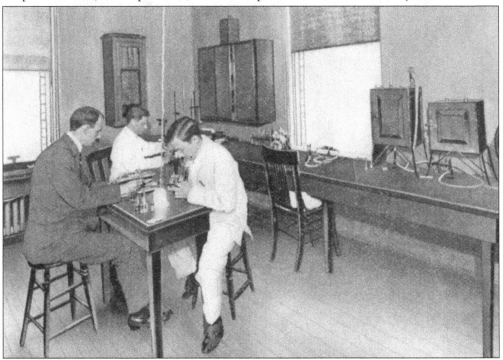

This photograph shows what was considered a well-equipped and spacious laboratory in 1909 in the newly opened Maurice Porter Memorial Pavilion on the south side of Fullerton Avenue. A microscope for the residents is being utilized here; in the background, a few Bunsen burners and probable microbiologic incubators can be seen on the bench.

Dr. Frank Spooner Churchill (1864–1946), an 1890 graduate of Harvard Medical School, was the most prominent CMH physician of this era. Specializing in diseases of children, he was president of the medical staff from 1909 until 1917, when he left for World War I as a major. Churchill was nationally prominent, publishing many articles on pediatric infectious diseases topics, serving as vice president (1902) and president (1916–1917) of the American Pediatric Society, the founding editor of the American Journal of Diseases of Children (1911–1918), and the chair of the AMA's Section on Pediatrics (1913–1914). He also established the first Infants' Clinic, held three mornings a week at CMH in 1917. After returning from World War I, Churchill devoted himself to public health in Chicago. During his tenure, the Otho S.A. Sprague Memorial Institute affiliated with CMH and supported research activities by one or two fellows and a director. Support from this institute has continued for 100 years, totaling $1.3 million from just 1993–2012.

Two very successful early women physicians were CMH medical staff members between 1909 and 1914. Pictured here is Dr. Gladys Henry Dick (1881–1963), a 1907 graduate of Johns Hopkins, who joined CMH as pathologist in 1912–1913, where she contracted scarlet fever. Later, she and her husband, George Dick, studied scarlet fever for decades at Chicago's McCormick Institute for Infectious Diseases (later the Hektoen Institute). In 1923, they isolated the causal hemolytic streptococcus, developed a susceptibility skin test, discovered scarlet fever toxin, produced antitoxin, and were Nobel Prize nominees in 1925. Dr. Grace Meigs Crowder (1881–1925) was first in her class as a 1908 graduate of Rush. Unfortunately, no adequate photograph is available. After studying abroad, she interned at Cook County Hospital (CCH), becoming attending physician at CCH and CMH, faculty at Rush, and fellow at the Sprague Memorial Institute at CMH. She was a CMH outpatient attending physician in 1911–1912, CMH pediatric resident in 1913, and an assistant attending physician in 1914. She joined the Labor Department's Children's Bureau in late 1914 in Washington, DC, as director of the Division of Hygiene until July 1918, and published a landmark 1917 study of US childbirth-related maternal mortality.

This street view, from around 1910, of the corner of Fullerton Avenue, Lincoln Avenue, and Halsted Street (looking north and west) captures the hustle and bustle of the growing city. Note the bus in the center of the intersection. No traffic light regulates the flow of vehicles. Just steps away from this intersection was the tranquil, parklike four-acre triangle of land that became the heart of the hospital campus after its 1904 purchase for $80,000. The view below, looking toward the northwest, shows the back (south) sides of the Agnes Wilson (left) and Maurice Porter (right) Pavilions that fronted on Fullerton Avenue. The grassy triangle area provided tennis and croquet courts, fresh air, and relative quiet within the busy city. At the rear of the Agnes Wilson Pavilion is a covered walkway leading to the isolation ward (hidden by the tree at left).

Funded by $125,000 from John P. Wilson, president of the Board of Directors (1904–1913), and $275,000 from others, the Agnes Wilson Memorial Pavilion, in the above photograph, facing north on the south side of Fullerton Avenue at Burling Street, opened in 1912 just west of the Maurice Porter Memorial Pavilion. It included nine wards, increasing hospital capacity to 175 beds, with space for administration, X-rays in the basement, Sprague Memorial Institute research labs, and an isolation pavilion to the south connected by a covered arcade. The outpatient department and dispensary moved here in 1913. At this time, brick walls were built around the campus triangle to protect equipment, tennis courts, and buildings. The photograph below, taken from the front of the 1886 building, shows the Maurice Porter (left) and Agnes Wilson Pavilions (right) across Fullerton Avenue. At the extreme right is the 1912 Aetna State Bank (later the Annex building) at Lincoln Avenue.

The above photograph, from about 1918, shows the southern facades of the isolation ward (far left) connected to the Agnes Wilson Pavilion (center), next to the Maurice Porter Pavilion (right), all opening to the parklike grassy expanse of the triangle. Many patients are scattered over the lawn on cots, receiving fresh-air therapy. The photograph below, from 1915, shows an outdoor class for mothers held in the shade of the isolation ward with its arcade connecting to the rear of the Agnes Wilson Pavilion. The location and design of the isolation ward helped to prevent exposure of the occupants of other buildings to highly contagious diseases. Physicians on the medical staff served as lecturers on various aspects of the care and feeding of children.

The multiethnicity of patients at CMH is apparent from these early photographs, in keeping with Julia Porter's desire for a facility to provide care without regard to race, creed, or ability to pay, which was quite unusual in that era. Many children suffered from tuberculosis of the spine (Pott's disease) or of other bones (tuberculous osteomyelitis), which were very common at this time, possibly including the young fellow in bed in the foreground of the photograph below, outdoors in the grassy triangle area. A wide variety of forms of tuberculosis, some pulmonary and many non-pulmonary, were reasons for prolonged (sometimes a year or even longer) hospitalization of children in the early decades of the hospital.

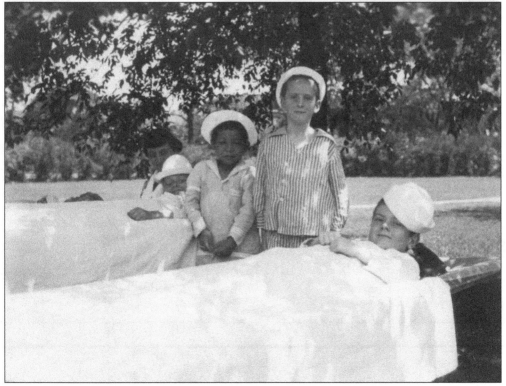

Seen in the photograph above, the Dow House on Orchard Street near the corner of Lincoln Avenue was one of the very few buildings on the mainly undeveloped triangle of land purchased in 1904. It initially served as a small outpatient clinic and dispensary in 1905; it then served as a nurses' residence together with two small, adjacent buildings in 1908 before becoming the interns' residence. It was demolished in 1933. The photograph below from 1918 shows a nursing school instructor and her student nurses. In 1918, at least two early nursing graduates succumbed to the great influenza epidemic. In the same year, five staff physicians, five resident physicians, three nurses, three nursing graduates, and the hospital X-ray technician/nurse anesthetist were all serving in World War I in Europe.

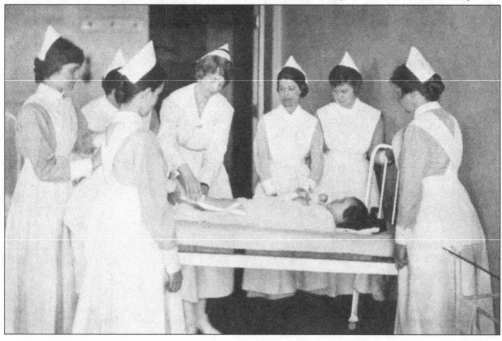

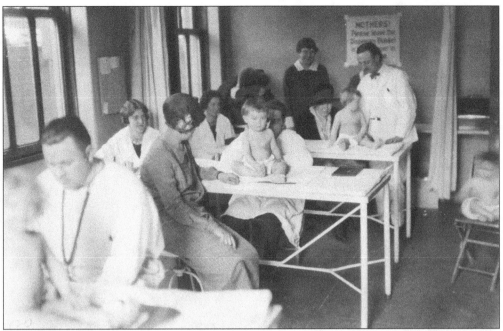

The outpatient department and dispensary (pharmacy), established in the Dow House, suffered chronically from lack of adequate space and became very crowded, as shown in the 1924 photograph above. The risk of potential transmission of infectious agents was substantial with patients so close together, and privacy was nonexistent. In 1908, the outpatient area and dispensary moved to the basement of the 1886 building before again moving to more spacious quarters in the Agnes Wilson Pavilion in 1913 and then ultimately to the Thomas D. Jones Memorial Building in 1940. Patient volumes increased dramatically over the years. Over 2,000 outpatient visits were recorded in 1908, but volumes increased strikingly to 4,500 in 1910; 18,000 visits in 1917; 27,000 in 1920; and 47,500 in 1930. Staffing was by interns and residents and many part-time voluntary physicians. The 1911 photograph below shows the ground-floor sunporch at the rear of the Maurice Porter Pavilion opening onto the triangle.

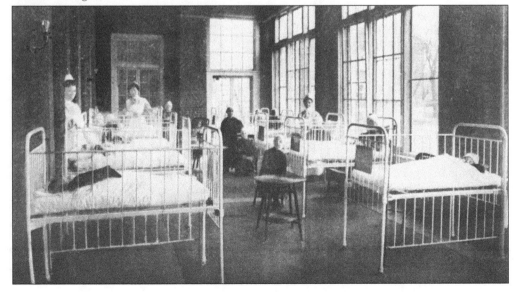

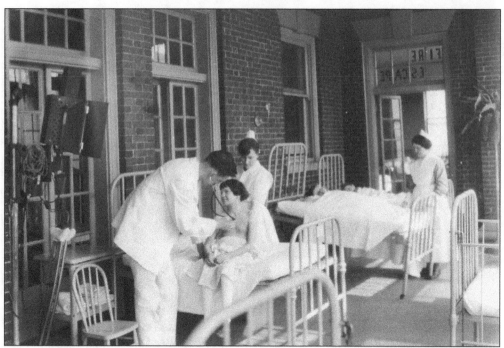

The cardiac ward, pictured here around 1920, mainly housed school-age patients, most with rheumatic fever and rheumatic heart disease, the illness to which 13-year-old Maurice Porter succumbed in 1881. These patients were generally hospitalized for up to six months while restricted to sedentary activity and treated with aspirin for its anti-inflammatory effect, with monitoring of the erythrocyte sedimentation rate. Dr. Stanley Gibson, who joined the CMH medical staff in 1920, established the first cardiology clinic at CMH in 1922 and became a national authority on rheumatic and congenital heart disease in children, later serving as chief of staff and chair of pediatrics at Northwestern University Medical School.

An early laboratory technician, seen here around 1920, has elaborate glass equipment and many chemicals with which to perform a relatively limited spectrum of investigations on patient specimens to aid in diagnosis and treatment. These included glucose and protein concentrations in spinal fluid, blood smears, Gram stains and basic cultures, and urinary studies.

The first telephone was installed at the hospital in 1894, initially with the number Lakeview 199. Prior to 1894, messages to the hospital were hand-delivered. An early hospital operator and her switchboard are pictured here around 1920. She represents the wide array of behind-the-scenes support staff essential to the functioning of the hospital.

John P. Wilson (1844–1922), a highly successful Chicago lawyer (right), served as a member of the CMH Board of Directors (1904–1922) and as president of the board during the important period of 1904–1913, contributing time and money very generously. He facilitated Julia Porter's gift for the Maurice Porter Memorial Pavilion (1908), provided $125,000 for the Agnes Wilson Memorial Pavilion in his daughter's memory (opened 1912), and gave more than $300,000 to the hospital endowment. His son (left), John P. Wilson Jr. (1877–1959), also contributed substantial time and money to CMH as a member of the Board of Directors (1907-1952), president of the board (1927–1952), and honorary board member until 1959. He also was a distinguished lawyer and major financial benefactor. His sister Martha Wilson's bequest in 1923 funded another major hospital building, the Martha Wilson Memorial Pavilion, which survived until 2012. John P. Wilson III (the infant in the photograph) and his wife also served on the Board of Directors. The John P. Wilson Society honors those who have made planned gift commitments to CMH.

Three

THE BRENNEMANN ERA
1921–1940

Dr. Joseph Brennemann (1872–1944), one of America's most respected pediatricians, served as the chief of staff at CMH from 1921–1940. Disappointed with the academic affiliation with the University of Chicago, he organized the teaching of Northwestern University Medical School (NUMS) students with Dr. Isaac A. Abt, NUMS pediatric chair, long before the formal 1946 agreement between CMH and Northwestern. The spectrum of hospitalized CMH patients in 1921 is preserved in a scrapbook of photographs taken by a resident that serves as a remarkable memoir from that era. Near the end of the Brennemann period, the first effective antibiotics (sulfa agents) dramatically impacted childhood infections.

During Brennemann's tenure, CMH's national profile was greatly enhanced, with substantial expansion of both physical facilities and physician staff. The estate of Martha Wilson funded construction of the 1926 Martha Wilson Memorial Pavilion, increasing capacity to 272 beds. Additional construction included the 1932 Nellie A. Black (NAB) Building as a residence for nurses and the 1933 Deering Building for interns on the site of the 1886 hospital. The Open Air Pavilion opened on the triangle in 1921 with funds generated by the White Elephant Rummage Shop. The power plant and laundry building on Lincoln Avenue opened in 1931, and a new outpatient building with an amphitheater, the Thomas D. Jones Memorial Building, opened in 1940.

Many important hospital staff additions were made during the Brennemann era. These included Drs. Albert H. Montgomery, chief of surgery (1920–1945); W. Stanley Gibson, who established Cardiology at CMH and served as NUMS chair of pediatrics (1939–1948) and CMH chief of staff (1944–1948); Willis J. Potts, the first full-time surgeon at CMH, chief of surgery (1945–1960); Paul Holinger, who established a world-famous Department of Bronchoscopy in 1935; John Bigler, director of the outpatient department (1932–1949), then CMH chief of staff and NUMS chair of pediatrics (1949–1962); and Archibald Hoyne, attending physician for contagious diseases (1922–1963).

Prior to the dramatic renovation of the central area of the triangle in the early 1960s, the large open area served many functions, with tennis and croquet courts for residents and nurses, and pastoral open-air meeting and play areas for convalescing patients, lectures to mothers and hospital staff, and other activities.

Dr. Joseph P. Brennemann (1872–1944), a 1900 graduate of Northwestern University Medical School (see diploma below), was CMH chief of staff (1921–1940) and in 1930 became CMH's first full-time salaried physician. Widely recognized as one of America's top authorities in pediatrics, he was president of American Pediatric Society (1929–1930), editor of a classic multivolume *Practice of Pediatrics*, and author of many scholarly papers. He was renowned as a clinician and teacher without peer and an international expert on infant nutrition. Brennemann substantially expanded CMH's physical facilities and physician staff, and in 1931, he brought another internationally recognized pediatric expert, Dr. Isaac A. Abt, NUMS chair of pediatrics (1909–1939), to CMH for teaching until 1942. Brennemann was known for his independent mind and reluctance to embrace unproven new theories without strong evidence. He documented the remarkable impact of the sulfa agents in the late 1930s, especially upon pneumococcal and streptococcal infections.

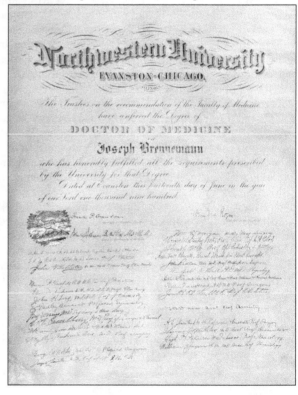

Pediatric interns and residents have trained at CMH since at least 1913. The eight predominantly male interns and residents of 1924 are shown in the photograph below with Dr. Brennemann (far left). Brennemann strongly supported establishment of a hospital library for residents, staff physicians, and nurses. In 1930, contributions from Mr. and Mrs. Richard Crane enabled the establishment of a library, which in 1940 was named the Brennemann Library. In the photograph at right, Brennemann (right) teaches while rounding with three residents in the Cribside Pavilion. One patient on Brennemann's rounds in 1939 was an eight-year-old girl with severe pneumococcal meningitis, who was treated with sulfanilamide and rabbit antisera and made a miraculous recovery. In 2012, at the age of 82, she contacted CMH to discuss her therapy and her recovery, and a progress note from Brennemann was found in her medical record.

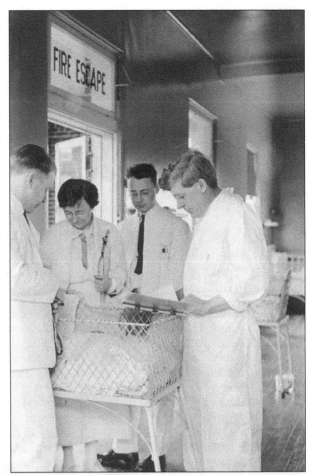

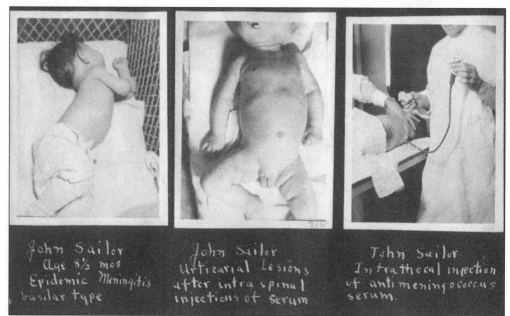

John Sailor
Age 8½ mos
Epidemic Meningitis
basilar type

John Sailor
Urticarial Lesions
after intraspinal
injections of serum

John Sailor
Intrathecal injection
of anti meningococcus
serum.

In 1921, Dr. Charles Eldridge, CMH pediatric resident, took more than 150 patient photographs, carefully mounting them in a scrapbook, and labeling with name, age, and diagnosis. This page shows three views of an 8.5-month-old boy. The left photograph shows the baby's abnormal posture secondary to epidemic (meningococcal) meningitis. The right photograph shows treatment with intrathecal (intraspinal) infusion of Flexner's horse anti-meningococcal antiserum, which lowered mortality of this infection from about 100 percent to about 13 percent. The middle photograph shows the recovered child with hives from serum sickness, a reaction to animal serum, that was generally not severe.

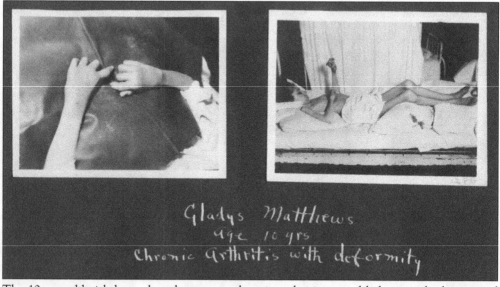

Gladys Matthews
age 10 yrs
Chronic arthritis with deformity

The 10-year-old girl shown here has severe chronic arthritis, most likely juvenile rheumatoid (idiopathic) arthritis (JRA or JIA). She has swollen fingers, wrists, knees with contractures, and marked loss of muscle mass. In this era, salicylate (aspirin) was the only somewhat effective therapy available.

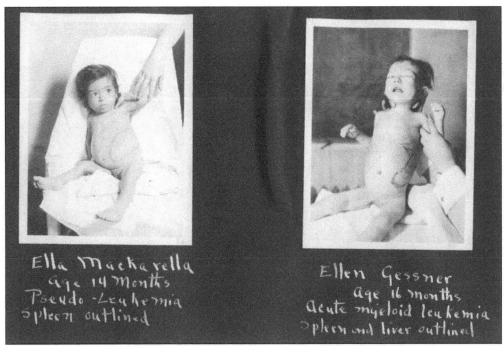

Ella Mackarella
age 14 months
Pseudo-Leukemia
Spleen outlined

Ellen Gessner
age 16 months
Acute myeloid leukemia
Spleen and liver outlined

Each of these girls has an enlarged spleen, and the one on the right also has an enlarged liver, as outlined on their abdomens. The child on the right apparently has acute myeloid leukemia, for which there was no therapy. The girl on the left has "pseudo-leukemia." She most likely has thalassemia, an inherited form of severe anemia that was not described until 1925 as Cooley's anemia.

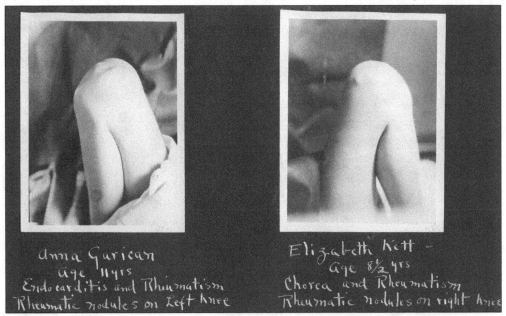

Anna Gurican
age 11 yrs
Endocarditis and Rheumatism
Rheumatic nodules on Left knee

Elizabeth Kett -
age 8½ yrs
Chorea and Rheumatism
Rheumatic nodules on right knee

Each of these two girls, 11 and 8.5 years old, has acute rheumatic fever with subcutaneous nodules over the knees. This is one of the most rare major features of acute rheumatic fever and is almost never seen in the United States today. This finding over extensor surfaces was particularly common in patients with fairly severe heart involvement related to rheumatic fever.

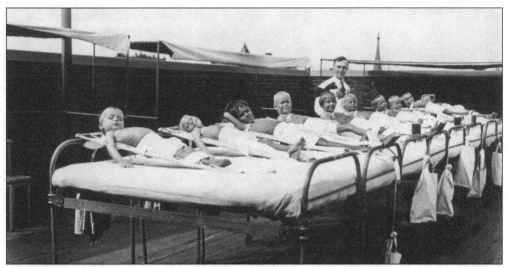

In 1922, a heliotherapy (sun therapy) facility was built on the roof of the Agnes Wilson Pavilion. Rows of children receiving heliotherapy are shown in both of these photographs, with the photograph below also showing the intersection of Fullerton Avenue, Lincoln Avenue, and Halsted Street in the far distance. Heliotherapy was very popular, especially for non-pulmonary forms of tuberculosis (spinal, bone and joint, abdominal, lymph node) as well as rickets (Vitamin D deficiency) and perhaps psoriasis. This therapy was pioneered by Dr. Auguste Rollier (1874–1954) in Europe, particularly in the Swiss Alps, where such facilities can still be found. Heliotherapy remained widely used until the late 1940s, when modern antituberculosis medications started to become available. Dr. Isaac Abt's 1924 pediatric text noted the germicidal and stimulating effects of sun exposure, stating that "climatic therapy is a valuable adjunct" in TB, and that heliotherapy speeds sequestrum formation in TB osteomyelitis, hastening healing.

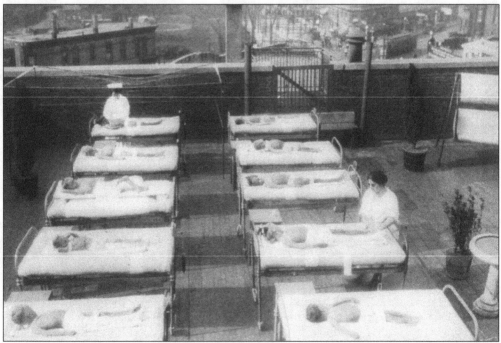

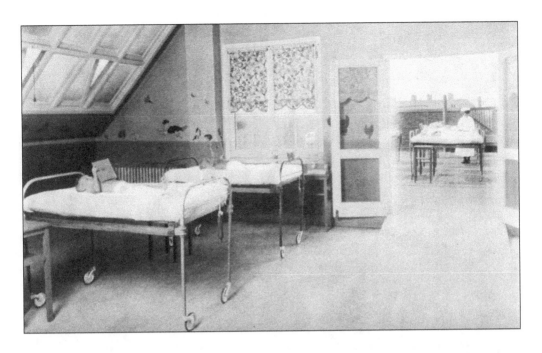

An indoor heliotherapy room housing 8–10 children was also built in 1922 on the roof of the Agnes Wilson Pavilion, with sloping glass windows that faced south to maximize sunlight (above photograph). This room opened to the rooftop itself for maximal exposure of children to fresh air and sunlight therapy as weather permitted. The initial Institute of Heliotherapy opened in 1903, centered around Leysin in the Swiss Alps near Lake Geneva. At its peak of popularity, Dr. Rollier ran 36 clinics with more than 1,000 beds in that area at 5,000 feet above sea level. In 1923, a *Time* magazine article credited Rollier and colleagues with having treated more than 2,000 children with bone and joint tuberculosis over 20 years, with an 80 percent cure rate.

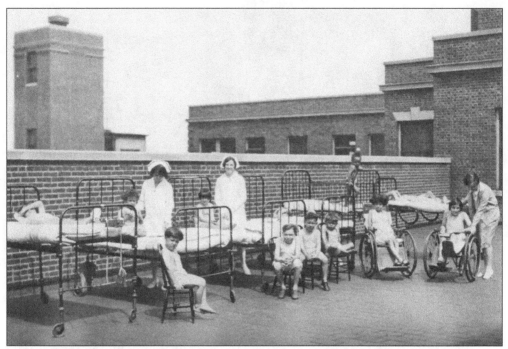

These additional photographs depict younger patients receiving heliotherapy at CMH, also known as climatic-therapy or helioalpine therapy. Heliotherapy is considered the oldest physiotherapeutic measure, dating to Herodotus in Greece in 431 BC and the Temple of Aesculapius at Epidaurus in ancient Greece. Many reports on this form of therapy were published in the 1910s and 1920s, including some with very impressive cure rates, such as 75 percent for vertebral or spinal tuberculosis, 90 percent for tuberculosis of the hip, 97 percent for tuberculosis of the knee, 94 percent for abdominal tuberculosis, 95 percent for tuberculosis of the lymph nodes, and 73 percent for TB of multiple bones and joints. Holt's 1936 *Diseases of Infancy and Childhood* considers heliotherapy the most valuable therapeutic strategy for the above forms of TB, and Nelson's fifth edition in 1950 indicates that "heliotherapy in moderation is of some benefit."

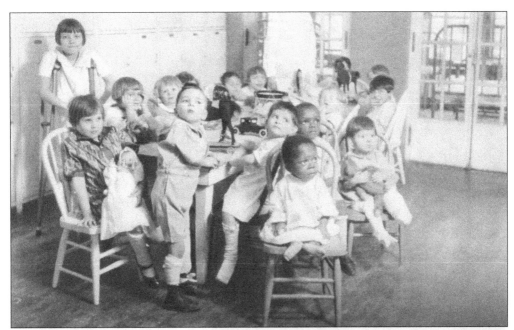

Dr. Edwin Ryerson (1872–1961), a graduate of Harvard in 1897, trained at Boston Children's Hospital, and was a consultant orthopedist at CMH (1906–1928), establishing the Division of Orthopedics. He was a national leader in orthopedics, president of the American Orthopaedic Association in 1925, first president of the American Academy of Orthopedic Surgeons in 1933, and NUMS chair of orthopedics (1929–1935). He was particularly interested in children with Pott's disease (spinal tuberculosis) and those with complications of polio. In 1982, his family funded the still-active Ryerson Fellowship in Orthopedics at CMH. The above photograph was taken on the orthopedic ward at CMH in 1926. This group of about 15 children includes some with crutches, casts, and braces. In this era, tuberculous osteomyelitis (bone infection) was extremely common, and Ryerson strongly advocated nonsurgical intervention whenever possible. Also common were bone conditions due to nutritional deficiencies, such as rickets and post-poliomyelitis sequelae.

Martha Wilson, daughter of John P. Wilson, president of the Board of Directors, was president of the Auxiliary Board, now called the Founders' Board, from 1911 to 1923. She donated the building that served as the original site of the White Elephant Rummage shop to the hospital in 1918. Upon her sudden death in 1923, she left her entire considerable estate to CMH, which funded construction of the 1926 Martha Wilson Memorial Pavilion on the southwest corner of Fullerton Avenue and Orchard Street, which included the first private beds (36). The Martha Wilson Pavilion, which remained until CMH moved in 2012, is shown here in 1930 with the Cribside Pavilion on Orchard Street to the south (left) and the Maurice Porter Pavilion on Fullerton Avenue to the west (right). The Martha Wilson Memorial Pavilion was remodeled in 1958, with an occupational therapy unit as well as cardiovascular and hematology laboratories.

Below, a 1925 view of the triangle looking north shows the isolation ward (which closed in 1914) attached to the Agnes Wilson Pavilion at the far left, the Maurice Porter Pavilion with the small Open Air Pavilion with columns (center left), the Martha Wilson Pavilion (center right), and Cribside Pavilion (far right), very nicely showing the considerable open space on the triangle. The image at right is a 1931 blueprint of the Children's Memorial Hospital campus oriented to conform with the photograph below to show the relationships among the buildings on the north and south sides of Fullerton Avenue, including the NAB and Deering Buildings (which are not visible in the image below).

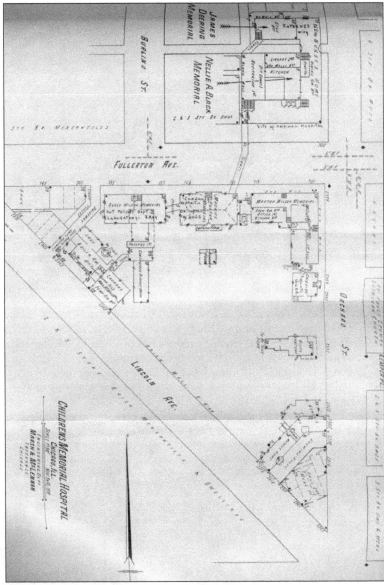

The White Elephant Rummage Shop opened in 1918 at 27 East Ohio Street in the brownstone deeded by Martha Wilson. The shop moved twice—once to 411 North LaSalle Street in 1953 and then to Lincoln Avenue and Halsted Street, across Lincoln Avenue from the hospital in 1960, closing in 2012 when CMH moved. Staffed by women from the Auxiliary (now Founders') Board, this used-goods shop raised funds, which were used initially to support several CMH projects, including construction of the Open Air Pavilion (1921). The photograph above shows crowds of people lined up to enter just before Christmas 1919, and the photograph below shows the fancy jewelry and silverware department of the White Elephant Rummage Shop in 1919.

In 1919, this small Ford truck was purchased to facilitate the collection of rummage items for the White Elephant Rummage Shop, primarily from the affluent and suburban North Shore. In this photograph from 1923, the truck is parked in front of the entrance to the Cribside Pavilion on Orchard Street (note the Bambino over the door); the east side of the Maurice Porter Pavilion is visible in the right background as the Martha Wilson Pavilion was not built until 1926. The White Elephant Rummage Shop had generated almost $2.69 million for the hospital by 1979 and in excess of $10 million by 2012. After covering the expense of the Open Air Pavilion, these funds were used mainly to support free care for patients and to support the Heart Center Fund.

The colonnaded Open Air Pavilion was opened in 1921 just behind the Maurice Porter Pavilion, but was not connected to any other building. It was built with funds generated by the White Elephant Rummage Shop. These views show that groups of patients were moved into this pavilion and participated in activities in the surrounding area, weather permitting of course. Some of the patients in the photograph below appear tanned, likely related to heliotherapy for tuberculosis infections.

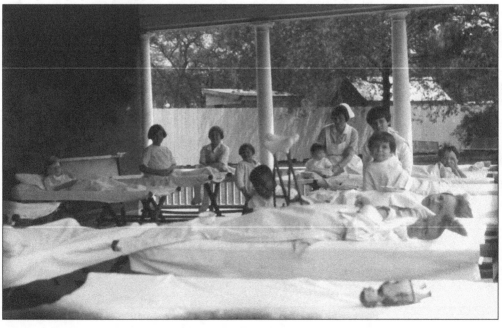

On nice days, the parklike area of the campus could be utilized for a class to instruct mothers about aspects of pediatric care, as in the photograph below, or for playing childhood games, or participating in a preschool-age nutritional class, as in the photograph above. The above photograph also nicely shows the southern (back) facades of the Agnes Wilson (at left) and Maurice Porter (at right) Pavilions, with the 1921 Open Air Pavilion just behind the Porter Pavilion. Dr. Brennemann was famous for his expertise related to infant nutrition, expressed in his writing and lectures on the topic. Studies by CMH staff physician Dr. Clara Davis, who examined nutritional habits of children hospitalized for long periods on the orthopedic ward, were highly regarded in the field. She was on the CMH staff from 1928 to 1958.

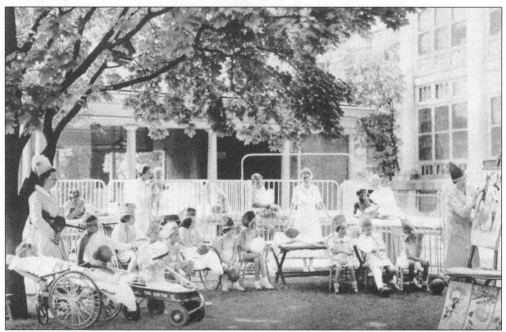

The central area of the triangle was used for many kinds of entertainment and therapy for the patients, including an art demonstration (photograph above) and a sandbox placed alongside the Open Air Pavilion with assorted vehicles (photograph below). These patients typically had extended lengths of stay, frequently 6 to 12 months—usually for various orthopedic conditions, bone infections, tuberculosis, or acute rheumatic fever, often with heart disease. Hospitalization was often indicated to improve nutrition, to provide fresh air and sunshine to promote healing, and to provide prolonged bed rest (as was standard for acute rheumatic fever).

Many children confined to beds or cots remained hospitalized to receive long-term physical and/or occupational therapy and were often moved to the triangle area for various activities. The image above shows patients along the east side of the Open Air Pavilion looking to the south, and the image below looks toward the west. In the distance in both of these photographs, the buildings across the street on the west side of Lincoln Avenue can be seen.

Dr. Albert Montgomery (1882–1948), a 1907 graduate of Rush, was on the CMH staff (1920–1948) and surgeon-in-chief at CMH (1920–1945) after serving in Europe in World War I. He was president of the Chicago Surgical Society and the Western Surgical Association, and a clinical professor of surgery at the University of Illinois. The photograph below shows the operating room at CMH around 1930, with the nurse-anesthetist at right, the X-ray view box, a nurse, and two surgeons. Surgery prior to the availability of antibiotics carried a high risk of infectious complications. As surgical cases became more numerous and increasingly complex, more extensive anesthesia coverage by physicians trained in anesthesiology was available, with Dr. William McQuiston serving as the first part-time attending anesthesiologist from 1951 to 1961, and Dr. David Allen serving as the first full-time chief of anesthesia in 1962.

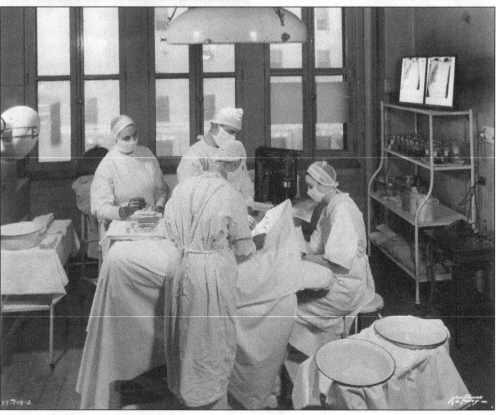

Dr. Archibald Hoyne (1878–1963), a graduate of Williams College in 1901 and Rush Medical College in 1904, served as medical superintendent of Chicago Municipal Contagious Disease Hospital (1922–1949) and attending physician and consultant for contagious diseases at CMH for over four decades (1922–1963). He was also chief of contagious diseases at Cook County, pediatric chair at St. Joseph's, and president of the Chicago Pediatric Society. One of the top US authorities on contagious diseases, particularly bacterial meningitis, Hoyne authored 67 articles on infectious disease topics and held professorships at the University of Chicago, University of Illinois, and Chicago Medical School. He documented the use of human convalescent scarlet fever serum to prevent and treat scarlet fever and to treat erysipelas, a severe Group A strep skin infection. He was also highly regarded for his student and resident teaching and meticulous patient care. Two interns and three lab techs are busy in the laboratory in the 1927 photograph below.

These two photographs, from 1915 (above) and 1923 (below), show how very crowded the outpatient department was prior to its relocation to the Thomas D. Jones Memorial Building in 1940. In 1923, the outpatient department volume had reached 30,462 visits by 17,544 patients, all receiving free care provided by a large number of volunteer staff physicians and residents. Despite efforts to exclude patients with highly contagious infections like measles (rubeola), chicken pox (varicella), and scarlet fever, the crowded conditions provided serious challenges and risked spread of these diseases. Outpatient volumes continued to climb in subsequent years. In 2012, the last year at CMH, there were 580,000 outpatient visits, including satellite clinics, and almost 99,000 emergency department visits.

These photographs show the Volunteer Motor Corps in action, bringing children to the outpatient department in the Agnes Wilson Memorial Pavilion on Fullerton Avenue and Burling Street around 1927. During that year, this group transported a total of 1,029 children and their mothers to the hospital. In addition, volunteers drove Social Service Department nurses throughout the Chicago area to make 4,539 home visits. The photograph below provides a nice view north along Burling Street; some of the buildings visible in the background of these photographs are still easily recognizable.

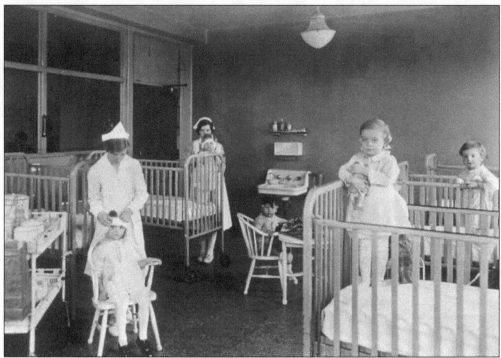

Like in many hospitals of the era, patients in the early 1930s were housed in multi-bed wards, each including about eight children and staffed by two nurses. Well-appointed single rooms and small wards for private (paying) patients, some with facilities for a parent to stay comfortably, were not available until the opening of the Martha Wilson Pavilion in 1926. The photograph below showing the older girls and an intern was taken in the cardiac ward, where most of the patients were very likely recovering from an episode of acute rheumatic fever, which today continues to be a common disorder in developing areas of the world but has become quite rare in the United States.

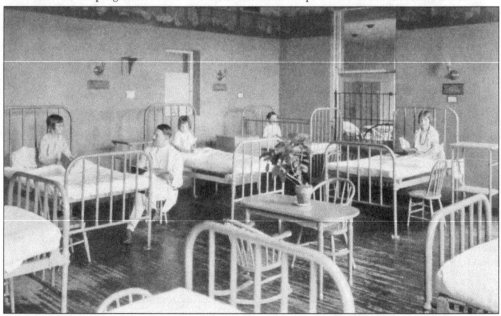

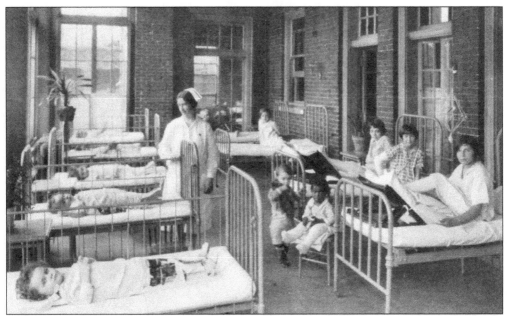

The image above from 1930 shows an orthopedic ward in the sunporch area of the Maurice Porter Memorial Pavilion facing the triangle. The photograph below shows the pneumonia ward, with children being treated with humidified oxygen in this pre-antibiotic era. Often, the pneumonia ward was kept quite cool with open windows as it was thought that fresh air (even cold air) was beneficial to these patients. One measure of medical progress was that the mortality rate of infants under 18 months who were admitted to the hospital declined, from 42 percent in 1928 to 9 percent in 1939, in large part due to the new sulfa antibiotics.

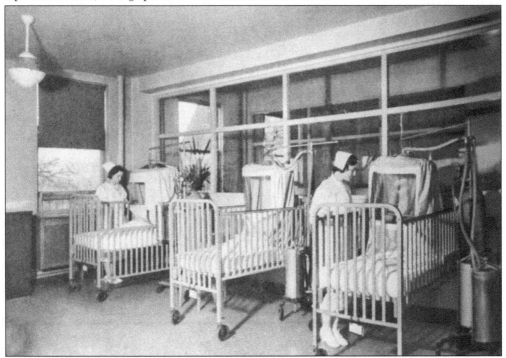

Hydrotherapy in a water-filled tank (above) was quite beneficial for helping to rebuild patient muscle strength. This was a particularly popular form of therapy for patients recovering from polio (paralytic poliomyelitis), as shown here. Polio epidemics continued to occur in Chicago into the 1950s, until the introduction of the first highly effective polio vaccine, Salk's injectable inactivated vaccine. Vaccine administration clinics were established at CMH and polio rates plunged in the late 1950s. Polio has been eliminated from the Western hemisphere for several decades and in the last several years has been limited to a handful of developing countries. The photograph below is an example of a different form of hydrotherapy, used for the treatment of superficial wounds such as burns. Both therapies are still used today.

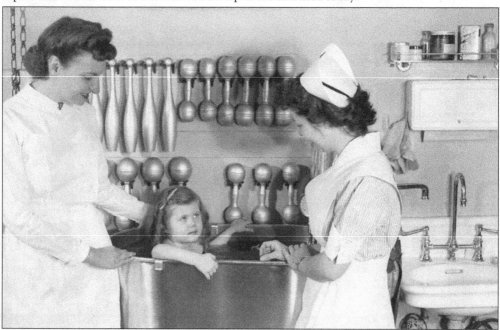

The photograph at right shows the Dental Clinic around 1928. This clinic was established in October 1917 in the Maurice Porter Pavilion; the first dentist was Dr. L.V. Magoon, an ancestor of Patrick M. Magoon, CMH president and chief executive officer since 1997. In 1917, it was noted that the annual cost of $360 to the hospital for the dental service "brought relief and lasting good to many children." Dr. Ray Jurado is the current chief of dentistry. The patient with the bandaged head and neck at the right in the photograph below most likely had undergone surgery for mastoiditis, infection of the mastoid area behind the ears. In 1935, prior to any antibiotics, 103 mastoiditis cases were treated surgically at CMH, with 2,016 hospital days (an average of 19.6 hospital days each) and six deaths. Ten years later in 1945, after the introduction of the sulfa agents and penicillin, there were only five mastoiditis cases, 81 total hospital days, and no deaths.

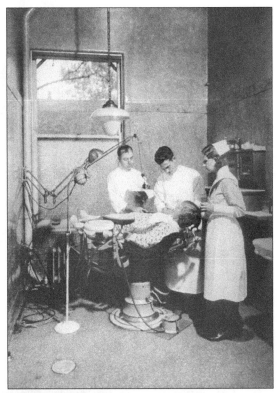

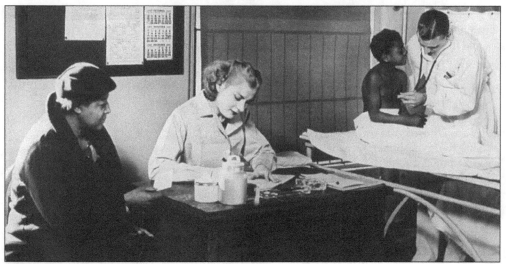

These photographs show the Diabetes Clinic, which was founded by Dr. Alvah Newcomb in 1930. This was nine years after the discovery of insulin by Dr. Fredrick Banting and Dr. Charles Best in 1921, which revolutionized diabetes treatment. The first patient was treated in 1922; sufficient quantities of purified insulin were available for patients within a few years. Newcomb was on staff at CMH from 1925 to 1960 and was president of the Chicago Diabetes Association in 1953. In 1949, he organized one of the first summer camps for diabetic children in the Midwest. Dr. Matthew Steiner (on the CMH staff 1939–1984) and Dr. Howard Traisman (on staff 1951–2004) were also instrumental in running this clinic and were recognized nationally for their expertise in diabetes in children. In the 1940 photograph at left, a clinic nurse instructs a diabetic child in self-administration of insulin.

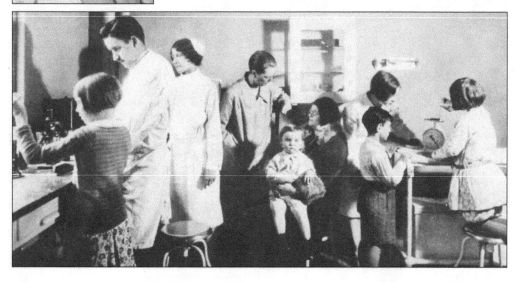

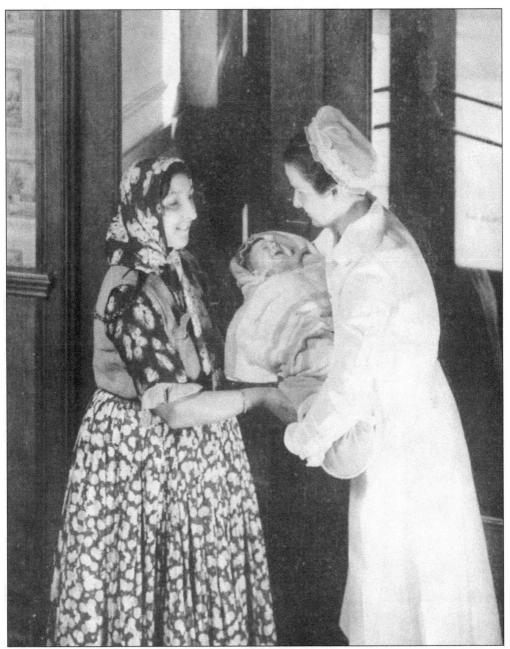

CMH provided care to countless children of immigrants, including the mother receiving her baby from the nurse in this 1938 photograph. The Great Depression years were particularly difficult for families with sick children, as exemplified by this 1934 letter: "I am so glad he got the attention of such splendid doctors and fine nurses. . . . I loved him dearly. . . . He had to starve and freeze when he was home—besides, I had to send him to the hospital with dirty clothes, hands, face, feet, etc. It looked like the child was neglected but don't you even think I would have done wrong to him. Here's the explanation—my gas was turned off, we had no coal, he begged and pleaded with me not to wash him in such ice water. I knew he was so weak from hunger that I didn't. . . . My heart is broken—it's so hard to lose a child and then to remember he was cold, hungry and dirty."

Dr. Isaac A. Abt (1867–1955) conducted teaching clinics and amphitheater presentations at CMH (1931–1942) for NUMS students and residents. One of America's most famous pediatricians, Abt was an international and national leader in pediatrics, holding many prominent professional positions, including serving as vice president and then president of the American Pediatric Society (1908–1909, 1927); founding president of the American Academy of Pediatrics (1930); longtime chair of pediatrics at NUMS (1909–1939); editor of the *Year Book of Pediatrics* (1902–1943); editor of the massive eight-volume pediatric text *Abt's Pediatrics*; chair of the White House Committee on Medical Care for Children (1930); chevalier of the French Legion of Honor (1927); and chair of the AMA Section on Pediatrics (1911–1912). He used the first diphtheria antitoxin in the Midwest (1895), was the first attending pediatrician at Cook County Hospital (1896), pioneered treatment of infant scurvy (1896), and was the first American to treat infantile diarrhea with milk albumin (1911).

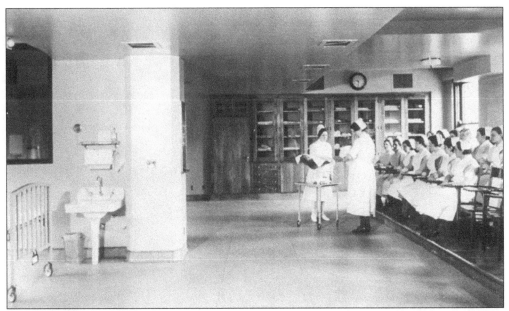

A training school for nurses was established at the hospital in 1894, graduating 10 nurses before closing in 1900 because of the lack of exposure to adult patients. A school of nursing opened again in 1908, this time providing two years of pediatric training and one year of adult training at Presbyterian Hospital. This was in addition to a short course in child nursing for students enrolled at a variety of nursing schools, which evolved to a focused 13 weeks of instruction in the nursing care of children. Shown above is a 1933 nursing class with a mock-up pediatric room at left. The photograph below shows the Nellie A. Black Building, which opened in 1932 as a nurses' dorm and was later utilized for office space and the psychiatric inpatient and outpatient areas.

These photographs show stages in the construction of the Thomas D. Jones Memorial Building on Orchard Street adjacent to the Martha Wilson Memorial Pavilion. The Thomas D. Jones Memorial Building was used mainly for outpatient clinics from its opening in 1940. This building was on the site of the original Cribside Pavilion, which was rebuilt on the triangle facing Lincoln Avenue. In the above view, looking northwest past the Jones construction site, one can see the southern (back) sides of the Agnes Wilson (left), Maurice Porter (center), and Martha Wilson (right) Pavilions. The photograph below, taken later from the east side of Orchard Street, shows the beginning of the connection with the Martha Wilson Pavilion at the right.

The completed Thomas D. Jones Memorial Building on Orchard Street is shown shortly after it opened in November 1940, attached to the Martha Wilson Pavilion at the far right. Thomas Davies Jones (1851–1930) succeeded John P. Wilson and preceded John P. Wilson Jr. as president of the Board of Directors, serving from 1914 to 1927, and served as a member of the board from 1903–1930. He supervised the development of several buildings on the CMH campus and contributed most generously to CMH, including a considerable sum in his will. The Thomas D. Jones Memorial Building included an amphitheater, isolation rooms, and areas for photography, X-ray, electrocardiography, medical records, pharmacy, dentistry, and the social service department. It was funded by a $600,000 gift from Jones's niece, Gwethalyn Jones, and $350,000 from Katherine Spencer Cramer, and closed only in 2012 when the hospital moved.

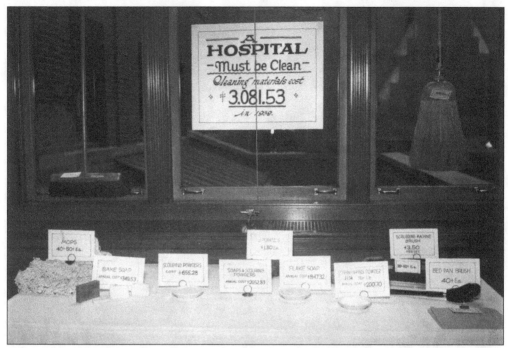

Behind-the-scenes activities at CMH involved many areas. Above, a display from 1939 highlights the costs of providing a clean environment at the hospital, totaling $3,081.53 in cleaning supplies that year. Below is the laundry area that provided cleaned and mended sheets, uniforms, gowns, and so forth for patients and staff. The building for the laundry and power plant (heating) opened in 1908 along Lincoln Avenue and was functional until the closing of CMH in 2012.

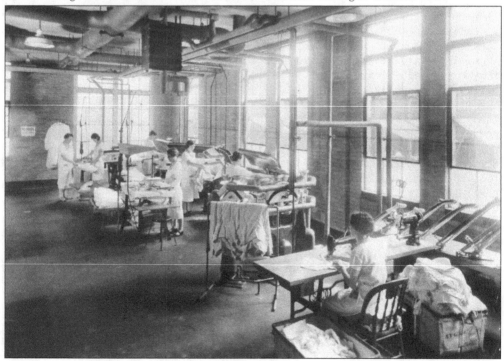

Four

WAR YEARS AND EXPANSION
1941–1962

Dr. Joseph Brennemann retired as chief of staff at the end of 1940. The onset of World War II in late 1941 created many challenges to CMH, including significant physician shortages and supply rationing. The transition to peacetime and the postwar years were notable for the return of many physicians and residents to prewar numbers, increased occupancy, and availability of research funds from the National Institutes of Health, National Science Foundation, and private foundations.

Medical leadership in this era included chiefs of staff Drs. C. Anderson Aldrich (1941–1943); Stanley Gibson (1944–1948), who established the formal affiliation between CMH and NUMS in 1946; and John Bigler (1949–1962). Dr. Willis J. Potts, pioneer blue-baby surgeon, became the first full-time chief of surgery (1945–1960), succeeding Dr. Albert Montgomery.

This era was also notable for the beginning of specialization within pediatrics, with the hiring of additional full-time medical staff including Drs. Harvey White in 1949 (radiology); Joseph Boggs in 1950 (pathology); Jerome Schulman in 1956 (psychiatry); David Hsia in 1956 (genetics and metabolism, chief of research); Irving Schulman in 1957 (hematology); Robert Miller in 1957 (cardiology); and Milton Paul in 1958 (cardiology), most with clinical and research activities.

In 1948, pediatrician Dr. Oliver Crawford became the first African American physician appointed to the medical staff; in 1950, African American nurses began to be hired, in part related to the large postwar migration from the South.

The postwar period was also marked by improved imaging and diagnostic techniques, and many medical and surgical advances, none more dramatic than the development of penicillin and other antibiotics, which had a striking effect on childhood morbidity and mortality.

By 1957, the need for CMH to undertake construction of a modern hospital building was clear to Bigler and administration. Although moving CMH to the NUMS campus was considered, it was decided that the hospital should remain in Lincoln Park, replacing the Maurice Porter and Agnes Wilson Pavilions and the parklike area of the triangle with a driveway from Fullerton Avenue to Lincoln Avenue (Children's Plaza), bed tower, administrative area, and connected research building. Chief of staff Bigler supervised the plans, with $5.5 million raised by philanthropy. Ground breaking occurred on November 1, 1960. The opening of the new buildings on October 11, 1962, marked a major transition for CMH.

Dr. C. Anderson Aldrich (1888–1949), on the CMH staff since 1922, succeeded Joseph Brennemann as chief of staff in 1941, leaving in late 1943 to direct a research project on preventative medicine at the Mayo Clinic. He held important positions with the American Pediatric Society, American Board of Pediatrics, and AMA Section on Pediatrics, and helped CMH through the difficult World War II period.

Dr. Stanley Gibson (1883–1956) served as chief of staff (1944–1948) and NUMS chair of pediatrics (1939–1948). Joining the CMH staff in 1921, Gibson established the cardiology department at CMH and became a national authority on congenital and rheumatic heart disease. He was vice president of the American Pediatric Society (1950–1951). Most importantly, in his dual role, Gibson was responsible for establishing the formal affiliation between CMH and NUMS in 1946 and guided the hospital through the rapidly changing postwar period.

Dr. Paul Holinger (1906–1978) established the bronchology department at CMH in 1935 and became a world leader in this field. A $17,500 gift in memory of four-year-old Edward Shedd Wells by his parents provided the necessary equipment, including a biplane fluoroscope, operating table, and instruments for state-of-the-art bronchoscopy; it also enabled Holinger's recruitment. Holinger served as chief of bronchoesophagology until 1974 and became president of many national and international societies in this field. In the photograph below, Holinger (center) is scoping a young boy diagnosed with a stricture (narrowing) of the esophagus after accidental lye ingestion, under fluoroscopic guidance, assisted by colleague Dr. Joyce Schild. Holinger's father was an early otolaryngologist in Chicago, and his son, Lauren, served as CMH chief of otolaryngology from 1987 to 2012. Philanthropic support by the Wells family and foundation to CMH has continued and has exceeded $4 million since 1936, including establishing the Paul H. Holinger, MD Professorship in Pediatric Otolaryngology.

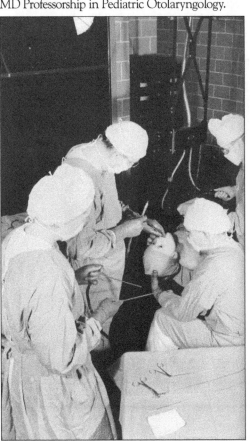

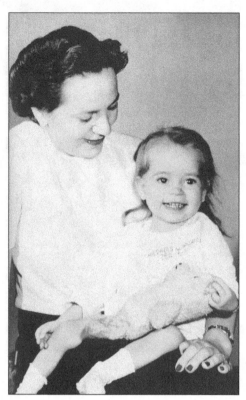

The child sitting on her mother's lap is 21-month-old Diane Schnell, who suffered from severe life-threatening cyanotic congenital heart disease (a so-called blue baby, related to the circulation of deoxygenated blood). On September 13, 1946, she became the first patient to undergo a historic aortopulmonary anastomosis by pioneer cardiac surgeon Dr. Willis J. Potts, aided by Drs. Syd Smith and Stanley Gibson, and made possible by a special vascular clamp developed by Potts. Diane had dramatic and immediate relief, left the hospital after 19 days, and survived 61 years until her death 2007. Patients from across the United States and beyond came to CMH for this lifesaving procedure, which antedated open-heart surgery by at least a decade. Potts received great international acclaim and performed 240 blue-baby operations within two years. He is pictured in surgery at the top left of the photograph.

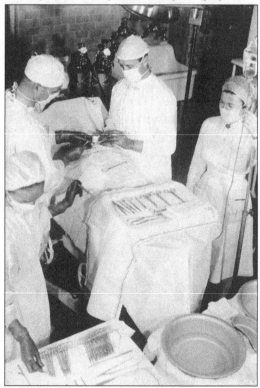

Dr. Willis J. Potts (1895–1963), a pioneer surgeon at CMH, became known internationally for his surgical creation of a direct aortopulmonary connection in severe cyanotic congenital heart disease. Shown above are Dr. Potts, the young Diane Schnell, and the dog Caesar, on whom Potts perfected his surgical technique. Potts served on the medical staff at CMH from 1930 to 1963 and was surgeon-in-chief from 1945 to 1960. He also served with distinction in both World Wars I and II. When Potts joined the CMH staff in 1930, there was only one pediatric surgeon in the United States; by his retirement in 1960, there were 75. Shown at left is a plaque from the National Society for Medical Research to commemorate "Caesar the Dog Hero." The Willis J. Potts Heart Center at CMH was established in 1964.

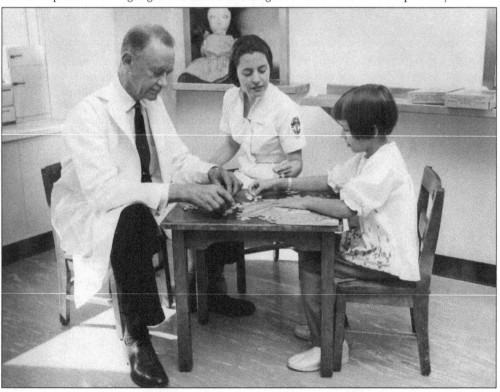

THE CHILDREN'S MEMORIAL HOSPITAL
707 FULLERTON AVENUE
CHICAGO 14
TELEPHONE DIVERSEY 8-4040
STATEMENT

7-7-53   19____

TO: Mr. Norman Wiltse

a/o Suellen

6/23 to 7/7/53	14 days @ 17.0			238	00
	Laboratory work			6	50
	Operating Room			32	50
	Solutions			4	25
	Penicillin			12	00
	Blood	23.25	Credit 17.50	5	75
	Oxygen			14	40
				$313	40

PAID

The Children's Memorial Hospital
CHICAGO, ILLINOIS

PLEASE DO NOT SEND CURRENCY THROUGH THE MAIL
SEND CHECK OR MONEY ORDER

FORM 53 7M
10-52

Willis J. Potts is shown playing a board game with one of his cardiac patients below. In the photograph above, a nurse walks with Suellen Wiltse (Miller), a 1.5-year-old patient with tetralogy of Fallot with a right aortic arch (a cyanotic congenital heart condition), who was operated on by Potts in 1953 and survived until 2011. The hospital bill received by Suellen's parents for the hospital stay, above, is remarkable for its simplicity and clarity. The contrast to modern health-care bills and expenses is most impressive and highlights the dramatic changes in health care over the past 60 years.

The dispensary (pharmacy) of the 1940s in the Thomas D. Jones Memorial Building is shown in the photograph at right with a large variety of medications. The photograph below is of a 1943 CMH "Support our Troops" display of some of the medications used by the armed forces during World War II, including quinine sulfate and quinine hydrobromide for malaria, sulfathiazole and sulfanilamide for bacterial infections, normal human plasma, morphine, and ascorbic acid (vitamin C). The war effort had great impact upon the hospital's functioning, creating personnel shortages, rationing of medication and supplies, regulations requiring specified work hours (at least 48 hours per week), blackout of windows, and others.

Dr. John A. Bigler (1896–1963) served as chief of staff and NUMS chair of pediatrics from 1949 to 1962, after having been a resident at CMH (1927–1929) and medical director of the outpatient department (1932–1949). He was also the director of the Otho S.A. Sprague Institute at CMH (1935–1949), and president of the American Board of Pediatrics (1961–1962). Bigler recognized the importance of research, and during his tenure he substantially expanded the full-time staff with mostly subspecialty clinician-scientists. He was also instrumental in converting CMH from a European pavilion-style hospital to a more modern facility that completely transformed the campus. Bigler's effectiveness was aided by the fact that he was pediatrician to the families of many members of the Board of Directors and Woman's Board. He died of cancer shortly before the new facility was completed. The 1962 cartoon below by Carey Orr of the *Chicago Tribune* serves as a fitting memorial.

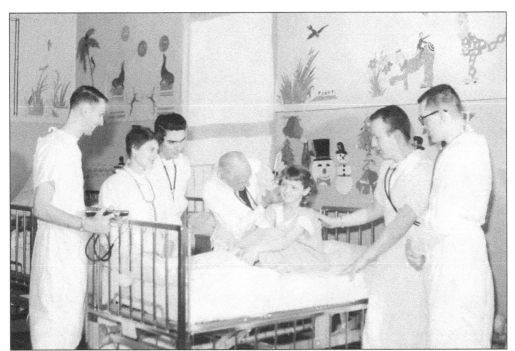

Dr. John Bigler was well known for his clinical and teaching expertise. In the photograph above, he is on clinical rounds with residents, doing bedside teaching. In the photograph below, at the Tumor Board in 1959, Drs. Bigler (center), Harvey White of radiology (at left), and Willis J. Potts of surgery (at right) discuss the case of five-year-old Kim, who was cured of a malignant liver tumor that was diagnosed at six weeks of age. Bigler also wrote that scarlet fever and its complications, including mastoid operations, had become rarely seen after the introduction of penicillin and that there was an 80 percent decline in the number of tonsillectomies as a result of antibiotics.

This 1944 drawing above shows the hospital campus at the time, with Fullerton Avenue running from bottom left to upper right and crossing Orchard Street in the foreground and Lincoln Avenue at the upper right. At this time, much of the most central portion of the triangle remained parklike. The 1942 layout below indicates the campus buildings and shows the full extent of the undeveloped area of the triangle. The new Cribside Building is the southernmost structure facing Lincoln Avenue, the original Cribside having been demolished to make room for the Thomas D. Jones Memorial Building on Orchard Street. Both photographs are oriented so that the Nellie A. Black and Deering Buildings are in the lower right corner. Over the next 20 years, the triangle was changed dramatically, with replacement of many of the buildings by a new bed tower, research building, and driveway.

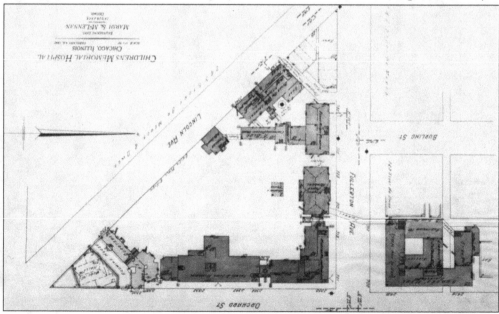

This aerial view (looking northwest along Lincoln Avenue, which runs from top to bottom at left) of the Lincoln Park campus in the 1950s shows the remaining, much smaller grassy area in the center of the triangle, the open parking lot built in 1955 on the triangle, and the Agnes Wilson, Maurice Porter, Martha Wilson, Thomas Jones, Nellie A. Black, Deering, and Cribside Buildings, as well as the laundry and power plant along Lincoln Avenue. Note the gas station and the Early Times Kentucky bourbon billboard at the corner of Lincoln Avenue and Orchard Street at the lower left. St. Paul's United Church of Christ on Orchard Street is clearly visible in the lower right area, and the edge of the DePaul University campus is at the top left corner. In its first 80 years up to 1962, the hospital had provided care for 222,074 inpatients and 625,338 outpatients, a very large proportion of which was free care.

Many activities continued to take place on the parklike open area until 1960, when construction began on that location for a new hospital tower and research building, including the Bigler Auditorium. The Open Air Pavilion is in the foreground of each view. Ambulatory and bedridden patients were often brought to this area for entertainment and recreation. Visiting animals, such as the horses seen here in the photograph below, commonly dropped by to entertain patients and staff.

Entertainment for the patients at Children's Memorial Hospital in the 1940s and 1950s included visits from the circus, complete with an elephant, chimpanzees, a clown, and a ringmaster. Shown here are a group of patients and caregivers at the Open Air Pavilion, with front-row seats for the show. The circus participants are on the open area of the hospital's triangle of land east of Lincoln Avenue and south of Fullerton Avenue, just behind the hospital's Maurice Porter and Agnes Wilson Pavilions, which faced north on Fullerton Avenue.

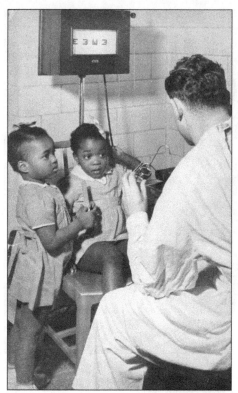

The image at left shows two children undergoing visual screening in the outpatient department in 1946. In that year, 8,101 patients registered for the outpatient department and they made 45,733 individual visits, including 1,097 patients who were seen in the Eye Clinic for 3,553 visits. The current ophthalmology chief is Dr. Marilyn Mets. The hospital's Social Service Department personnel also made 1,006 home visits. The photograph below shows Dr. Alan Siegel screening children's throats in the very crowded streptococcal clinic in the late 1950s. In that era, acute rheumatic fever was still a major threat to US children. This complication of strep throat was studied extensively at Children's Memorial Hospital in the 1950s and 1960s by Siegel, Dr. Gene Stollerman, and colleagues. In 1991, the lounge of the Nellie A. Black Building was the site of a historic meeting of the American Heart Association's committee to revise the classic Jones Criteria for the diagnosis of acute rheumatic fever.

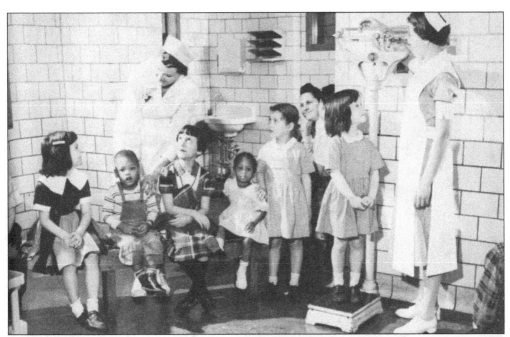

The outpatient clinics at CMH in the 1940s were very active, with the number of patients and clinic visits increasing steadily. The hospital's annual report for 1947 notes that 63 percent of all medical, surgical care, and hospitalization costs were provided free to patients; in 1958, the cost of free care exceeded $1 million for the first time. The hospital's endowment income and receipts from patients was inadequate, and the hospital's budget was highly dependent each year upon philanthropic support and assistance from relief agencies and the Community Fund. Medical clinics included allergy, cardiac, dermatology, diabetic, endocrine, hematology, infant, luetic (syphilis), medical, nephritic, neurology, and speech clinic—the two largest being the medical clinic, with 23,208 visits, and the infant clinic, with 4,627 visits. Accurate height and weight measurements, as illustrated in the photograph at right, are, of course, key to assessing growth and development of children.

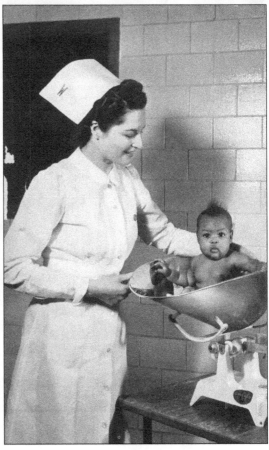

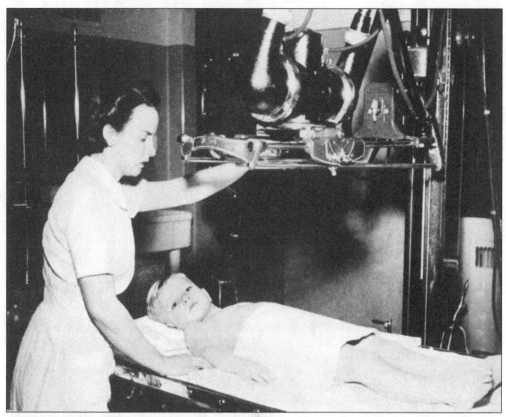

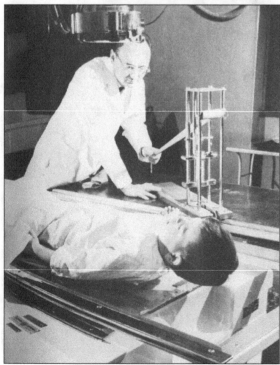

During the 1940s (photograph above), radiologic services were provided by a nurse-technician and a part-time radiologist, Dr. William Anspach, who served from 1931 to 1949. Dr. Harvey White (photograph at left) became the first full-time radiologist in 1949 and was chief of radiology from 1949 to 1979, becoming a national leader in pediatric radiology. He was succeeded as chief by Dr. Andrew Poznanski (1979–1999) and then by Dr. James Donaldson (1999–present). The Department of Radiology changed its name to the Department of Medical Imaging in 2000.

This operating room photograph at right, from the late 1950s, shows a child undergoing spinal surgery. The child in the photograph below is in a Risser frame for the placement of a body cast following spinal surgery. Advances in pediatric anesthesia, pediatric imaging techniques, and antibiotic therapy all contributed to improved surgical outcomes. Outpatient surgical clinics included dental; ear, nose, and throat; eye; orthopedics; plastic and oral surgery; general surgery; and urology. The busiest of these clinics in 1947 were the eye clinic (3,746 visits) and the general surgery clinic (3,098 visits).

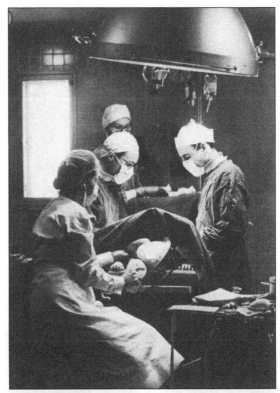

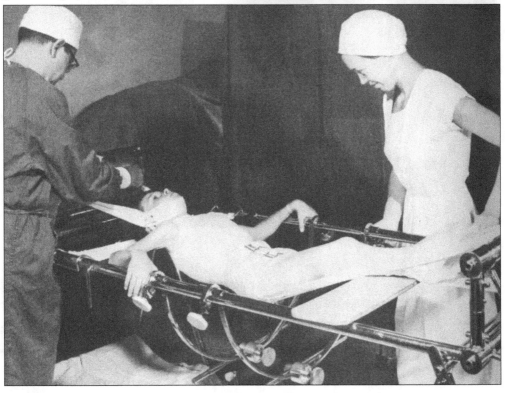

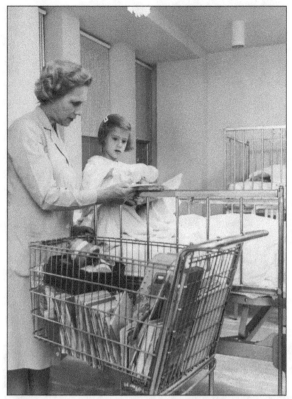

The education of hospitalized patients was long an active priority at Children's Memorial, with a kindergarten beginning in 1893 and the regular provision of teachers dating back to about 1912, supported by Augusta Nusbaum Rosenwald. In the photograph below are four children in a reading lesson with a teacher. In the photograph at left, the portable library delivers books to a patient. The *History of Medicine and Surgery of Chicago* (1922) notes that convalescent patients at CMH received four hours per day of instruction by two teachers so that they would become "adept at basket weaving, knitting, and sewing." Fortunately, there were also classes in reading and writing for older children and "suitable instructive games for younger children." Since 1923, teachers for the hospital have been supplied by the Chicago Board of Education; in 2012, two Chicago Public Schools teachers provided education for patients.

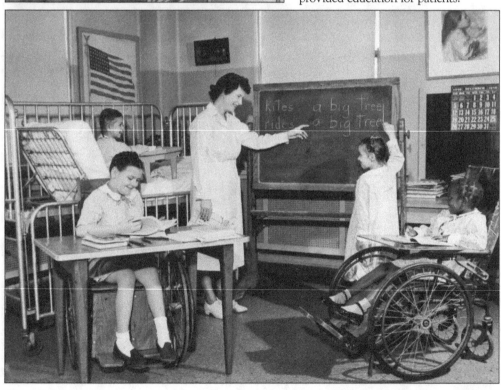

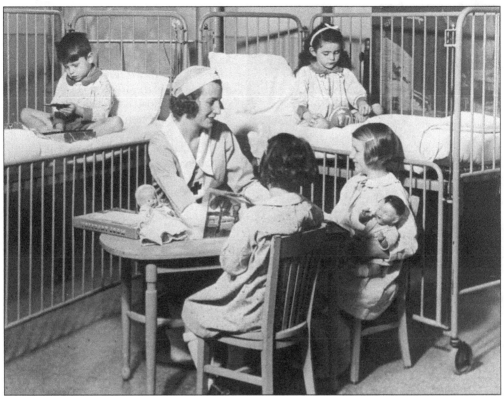

The children pictured here highlight play therapy. Julia Porter viewed the nonmedical aspects of treatment as important for the care and cure of children. She ensured that patients had books, art, education, and entertainment. In 1904, the volunteer Cribside Society raised funds to "furnish amusement for convalescent children in the hospital," and in 1932, CMH hired the first paid supervisor for recreation. This function more recently has become the responsibility of the Child Life Department, involving professionals as well as many volunteers.

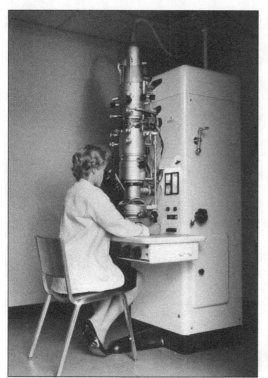

The photograph at left shows a technician operating an early transmission electron microscope around 1960. This was used for both clinical and research purposes to greatly magnify objects, enabling visualization of intracellular structures. The photograph below shows a child's breathing dynamics being monitored by a smoked drum kymograph, which was developed by Carl Ludwig in 1847 and was still being utilized to measure respiratory motion, heart rates, and muscle contraction in the early 1940s. This early technology has, of course, been supplanted by infinitely more sophisticated methodologies today. This child may have cystic fibrosis, a common genetic disorder that affects lung function. CMH has had its Cystic Fibrosis Center since 1963, initially headed in succession by Drs. David Hsia, Margaret O'Flynn with William Rowley, Pete Gibson, Hans Wessel, and most recently Susanna McColley, head of the Division of Pulmonology. The center provides comprehensive care for patients with this significant illness.

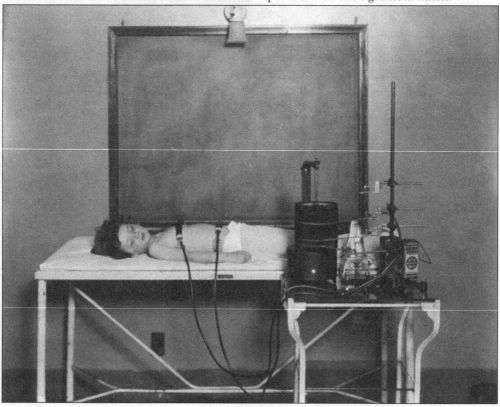

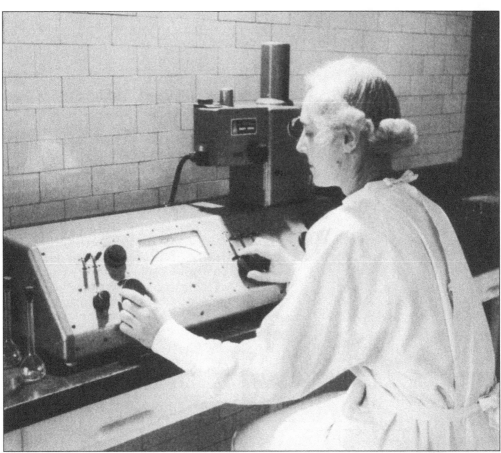

In the photograph above, the 1952 state-of-the-art spectrophotometer for chemical analysis of the blood, including electrolytes, represents a significant diagnostic laboratory advance based upon absorbance of light at various wavelengths. The understanding of fluid and electrolyte balance began around 1925 and improved over time, contributing substantially to lower mortality rates, especially of infants under two years of age. Total laboratory procedures increased from 43,000 in 1947, to 105,000 in 1957. In the photograph at right, a child in the late 1950s undergoes a radioactive thyroid scan in the early days of nuclear medicine scans for diagnostic purposes.

The photograph at left from 1945 shows the application of an intradermal skin test for tuberculosis in the outpatient clinic. This is still a highly effective tool to diagnose latent or active tuberculosis. In the 1940s, tuberculosis continued to be a very common, serious, and difficult to treat illness. For example, in 1943, four children with tuberculous bone infection were hospitalized at CMH for a total of 1,463 days (an average of a one-year hospitalization for each), seven with pulmonary (lung) tuberculosis for a total of 123 days, and four infants under two years with tuberculous meningitis for a total of 107 days, but all four died. In the photograph below, a child with earphones is undergoing audiologic testing in the updated audiology room facilities at CMH built in 1953. Hearing aids and, much later, cochlear implants for children with severe hearing disorders were pioneered at CMH, the latter by otologist Dr. Nancy Young.

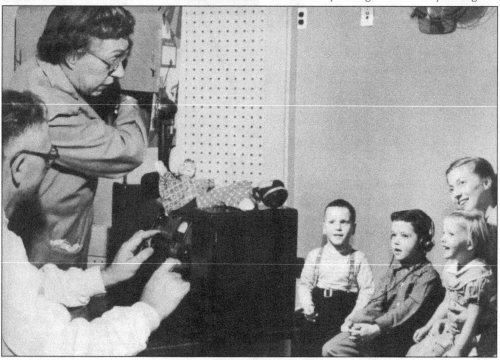

In the 1940s and 1950s, polio was a serious threat almost every year, with large numbers of patients admitted to CMH for convalescent care. The year 1951 saw a particularly large polio epidemic. The photograph below shows two post-poliomyelitis siblings, Kathy and Mark, receiving physical therapy. In the photograph at right, a polio patient is being retaught to use his arms. The importance of polio vaccine to prevent this crippling disease was emphasized at CMH when it became available, with large numbers of doses administered in the clinics beginning in February 1956. This killed injectable Salk vaccine was later supplanted by the live attenuated oral Sabin vaccine, which was in turn replaced later by the injectable Salk vaccine.

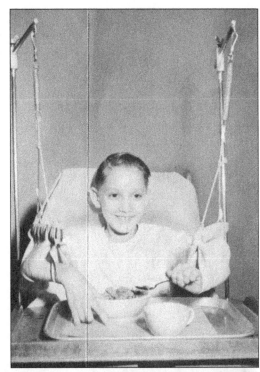

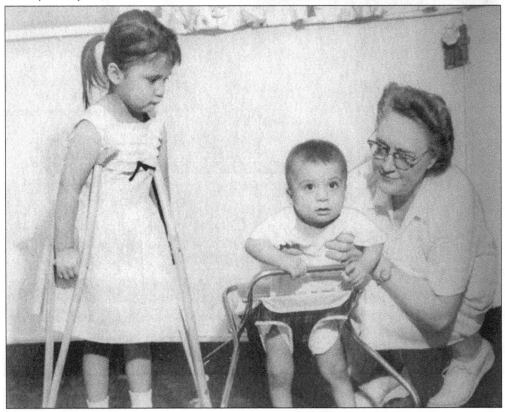

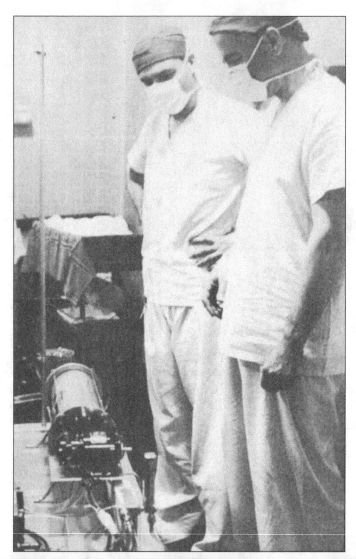

In the photograph at left, Dr. Willis J. Potts (right) and a colleague in the operating room in the late 1950s inspect an oxygenator, an early version of a cardiac bypass device, which provided adequate oxygen during heart surgery. In the photograph below, a cardiac catheterization with cineangiography is being performed as a cooperative effort between cardiology and radiology in the 1950s. The Congenital Heart Disease Clinic opened in 1952, and in 1959 a two-year cardiology fellowship was established. Innovative complex cardiovascular surgery at CMH continued over the decades, including Dr. Thomas Baffes's 1955 partial venous switch procedure for transposition of the great vessels (which became the standard procedure worldwide for many years), Dr. Farouk Idriss's 1984 use of pericardium to repair complete tracheal rings, and repair of congenital vascular rings by Drs. Carl Backer (CV) and Lauren Holinger (ENT) in the 1990s and 2000s.

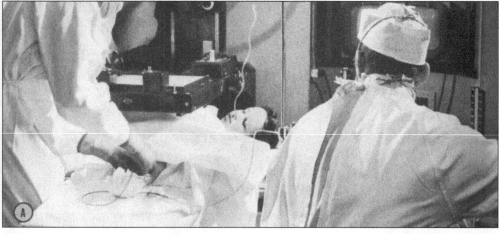

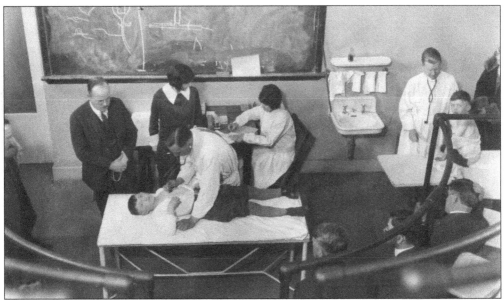

In the photograph below, Dr. Milton Paul presents data at a cardiology conference in the amphitheater of the Thomas D. Jones Memorial Building in the late 1950s. Behind and to his left in the business suit is Dr. Robert Miller, the first full-time chief of cardiology at CMH (1957–1963). In 1957, a new cardiovascular lab opened in the basement of the Jones Building, equipped for cardiac catheterization and including television monitors. Paul was on the medical staff from 1958 to 1993 and served as chief of cardiology from 1963 to 1984. In the photograph above, several children are lined up for examination by visiting cardiologists. The amphitheater was heavily utilized for teaching conferences and other activities.

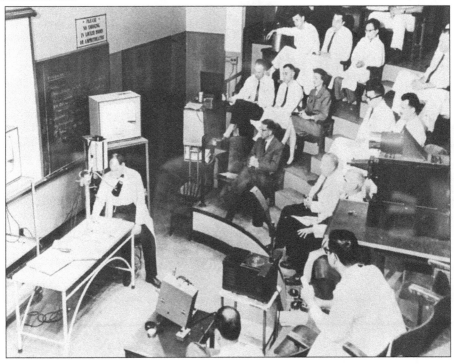

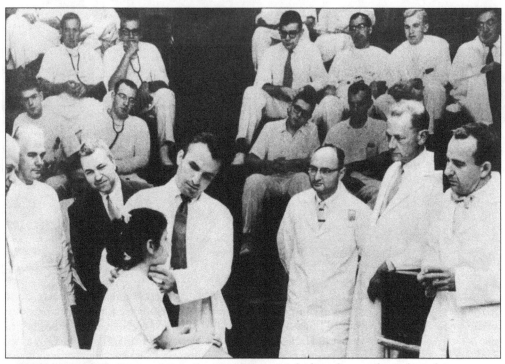

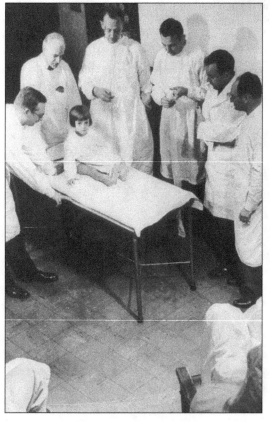

Multidisciplinary clinical teaching conferences in the amphitheater, including the Tumor Board, where the cases of children with cancers were discussed, are shown in these photographs from the late 1950s. The Tumor Board was established in 1951. In the above photograph, Drs. Bigler (far left), White (third from right), Potts (second from right), and Boggs (far right) participate, representing pediatrics, radiology, surgery, and pathology, respectively. The same physicians are identifiable in the photograph on the left. This highly multidisciplinary conference brought together a wide range of specialists (prior to the availability of many subspecialists) to evaluate and discuss patients and to educate students and residents about clinical disorders.

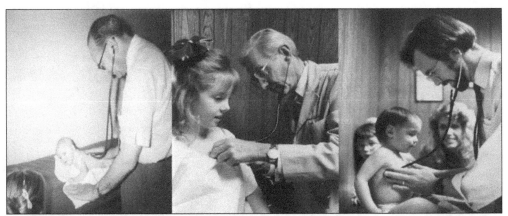

This triptych shows three generations of Traisman pediatricians who served on the medical staff of CMH from 1941 to 2012. Dr. Alfred Traisman established the North Side pediatric practice in 1923 and joined the staff in 1941; his son Howard served on the staff from 1951 to 2004 and was president of the medical and dental staff in the 1970s; Alfred's grandson Edward has been on staff from 1984 to present, also serving as president of the medical and dental staff from 2011 to 2012. Dr. Howard Traisman was an internationally recognized authority on juvenile diabetes and coauthored a text on the topic with Dr. Alvah Newcomb in 1965, then revised it in 1971 and 1980. He was the first recipient of the CMH Distinguished Service Award.

Numerous faculty members have contributed to the CMH teaching programs over the years. Among the most noteworthy are the "Bobs"—Drs. Robert Listernick (left) and Robert Tanz (right), of general academic pediatrics, with more than 65 combined years of outstanding teaching and mentorship. Bioethicist Dr. Joel Frader is the current chief of general academic pediatrics. Dr. Sharon Unti has directed the pediatric residency program since 1994.

On November 1, 1960, three CMH patients (each with a small steam shovel) joined the presidents of the Board of Directors and the Woman's Board—Hughston McBain and Mrs. Chauncey Keep Hutchins—and the chairs of the Development Drive to break ground for the new hospital and research buildings. The photograph below from 1962 shows the very early stage of demolition of the Maurice Porter Pavilion on Fullerton Avenue, with the newly completed bed tower looming in the background. Over $5.5 million in philanthropic support from the community at large and from long-term donors to the hospital was critical to this transformative construction project.

These two 1961 photographs were taken during the construction of the new bed tower and research building. The photograph above (view looking west) shows Lincoln Avenue at the left and Children's Plaza (the driveway), under construction, running horizontally across the foreground to connect Lincoln Avenue to Fullerton Avenue. The photograph below (view looking north) shows the foundation of the bed tower, with the south facades of the Agnes Wilson (left), Maurice Porter (center), and Martha Wilson (right) Pavilions in the background. The challenges of running an active children's hospital at close to its usual capacity in the midst of such extensive construction seem quite daunting.

These photographs from the early 1960s show the north (above) and south (below) aspects of the recently opened driveway (officially Children's Plaza), with the new bed tower and research building in the background. The new bed tower opened on October 11, 1962, although the first patients moved in on March 31, 1962. The research building opened in 1963. A symposium honoring Dr. John Bigler was held on October 10, 1962. At the far right in the lower image, the area just to the right of the driveway is the future site of the Kroc Building, which would not be erected for another 20 years.

This ground-level view over the outdoor parking lot in 1962 shows the newly completed bed tower (center, background) with the research building (left center, in front of the bed tower), and the Bigler Auditorium (left). The older Martha Wilson Memorial Pavilion is at the right. This construction transformed the classic-style pavilion hospital model into the modern unified hospital bed tower. The campus on the triangle was nearing its final configuration, with the exception of the outdoor lot. Four additional floors were added to the bed tower in 1982. Parking in busy Lincoln Park was likely an ongoing issue over many decades.

The opening of the new bed tower in 1962 was celebrated in this daring (but unsafe?) publicity photograph with 10 patients and 10 nurses. In 2002, CMH began an educational campaign called Stop the Falls to help prevent window falls by children in the community, which were increasing. Because injuries are the leading cause of death and long term disability among children 1–19 years old, in 2005 the Injury Prevention and Research Center was established at CMH to coordinate hospital child advocacy activities that focus on the prevention of intentional and unintentional injuries to children. These activities range from promoting the value of safety helmets to child abuse prevention—by fostering protective environments, improving public policies, enhancing knowledge and skills, and increasing awareness—under the medical leadership of Dr. Karen Sheehan. This center collaborates with many hospital services and offices, including the Office of Child Advocacy and the Mary Ann and J. Milburn Smith Child Health Research Program.

Five

TO THE CENTENNIAL
1962–1982

This 20-year period leading to the CMH Centennial saw steady growth of pediatric and surgical services, the addition of full-time staff over an expanding spectrum of childcare specialties, expansion of research facilities and funding, and development of educational programs with NUMS. Pediatrics was led by Drs. Robert Lawson (1962–1970) and Henry Nadler (1970–1981); both also served as chief of staff. Surgery was led by Drs. Orvar Swenson (1960–1973) and Lowell R. King (1974–1981). From 1967 to 1973, relocating CMH to the NUMS campus again received serious consideration; the Board of Directors voted in 1970 and again in 1973 to remain in Lincoln Park.

The first two professorships at CMH were endowed by the Irene Heinz Given and John Laporte Given Foundation in 1968, with Drs. Henry Nadler and later H. William Schnaper occupying the Irene Heinz Given and John LaPorte Given Research Chair in Pediatrics. The Irene Heinz Given and John LaPorte Given Chair in Pediatrics has been held by Drs. Robert Lawson, Wayne Borges, Robert Winter, and, currently, Ellen Chadwick. Two additional endowed chairs were established around 1978: the Martha Washington Home Chair in Orthopedics, held by Drs. Myke Tachdjian and John Sarwark, and the A.C. Buehler Chair in Cardiovascular Surgery, held by Drs. Farouk Idriss, C. Mavroudis, and Carl Backer.

Highlights of this era included opening the research building in 1963, NIH funding the CMH Clinical Research Center in 1964, and research grants exceeding $1 million by 1964. The transplantation era began in 1964, with the first kidney transplant performed by Drs. Farouk Idriss and Orvar Swenson. Major physical expansion in 1981 resulted from the $50 million Centennial Fund with a large gift from Ray and Joan Kroc to build the Diagnostic and Treatment Center.

From 1960 to 1970 to 1980, full-time physicians increased from 12 to 47 to 115, reflecting increased patient numbers and complexity. From 1970 to 1980, nursing staff increased from 377 to 613. Many new pediatric and surgical divisions were established in the 1970s. Dermatology, for example, has provided world-class care and teaching since 1979, led by Drs. Nancy Esterly, Amy Paller, and, most recently, Anthony Mancini. Dramatic changes in financing of medical care characterized this era. From originally providing mainly free care, CMH's reimbursement from new federal programs rose from $23,000 (1945) to $177,000 (1954) to $2.5 million (1968). In 1966, CMH established Near North Clinic with Chicago Board of Health and US Children's Bureau funding to serve neighboring communities.

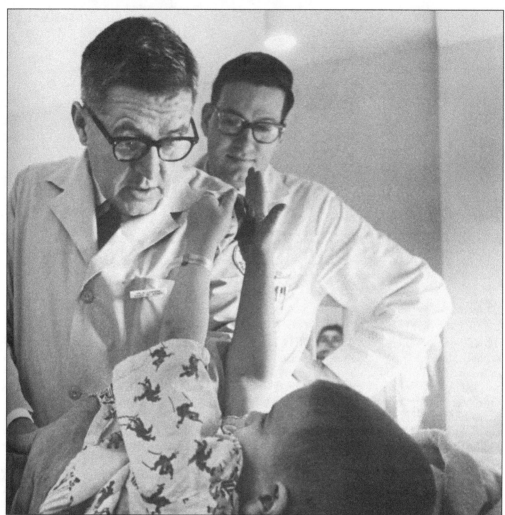

Dr. Robert Lawson (1911–1996), a 1936 graduate of Harvard Medical School, was recruited from the University of Miami to replace Dr. John Bigler as chief of staff and NUMS chair of pediatrics. He served from 1962–1970, when he became vice president for Health Sciences at NUMS. Lawson was secretary-treasurer (1957–1958), vice president (1960) and president (1968–1970) of the American Board of Pediatrics, and editor of the *American Journal of Diseases of Childhood* (1954–1957). Early in his tenure, he established and recruited leadership for many new divisions: infectious diseases, Dr. Hugh Moffet; hematology, Drs. Wayne Borges and, later, George Honig, Sharon Murphy, and Morris Kletzel; endocrinology, Drs. Orville Green and, later, Bernard Silverman, and Don Zimmerman; allergy, Drs. Gilbert Lanoff and, later, Richard Evans and Jacqueline Pongracic; neurology, Drs. Gordon Millichap and, later, Marianne Larson and Leon Epstein; urology, Drs. Lowell King and, later, Casey Firlit and William Kaplan; orthopedics, Drs. Mihran Tachdjian and, later, John Sarwark; student teaching, Dr. Floy Helwig; and clinical research center, Dr. Tom Egan. Lawson was considered a superb teacher and clinician.

Dr. Orvar Swenson (1909–2012), became surgeon-in-chief in 1960, serving until 1973. A native Swede, he grew up in Missouri, graduated from Harvard Medical School, and trained in surgery at Harvard and in pediatric surgery at Boston Children's Hospital from 1945 to 1949. After establishing pediatric surgery at Tufts (Boston Floating Hospital) from 1949 to 1960, Swenson was recruited to CMH to succeed Dr. Willis J. Potts. Swenson became world-famous for his innovative Hirschsprung's disease surgery and research on this very serious congenital bowel disorder. He served as president of the American Pediatric Surgical Association (1964–1965), received many awards, and edited a classic text on pediatric surgery, which he revised several times. During his tenure as surgeon-in-chief, he expanded surgical services substantially, including renal transplantation. Swenson died in 2012 at the age 103.

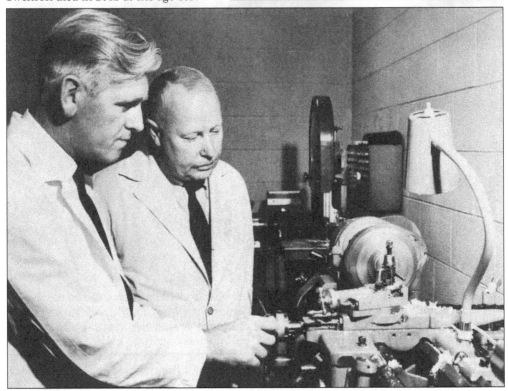

Key figures in the establishment of substantial research programs at CMH were Drs. David Y.Y. Hsia (1925–1972), at left, and Henry Nadler, below. Hsia trained at Boston Children's, joined the CMH staff as chief of genetics and metabolism (1957–1969), and served as CMH's first director of research (1958–1969). He received the prestigious E. Mead Johnson Award from the Society for Pediatric Research in 1965 for his classic studies of phenylketonuria (PKU). Dr. Joel Charrow is the current chief of genetics and metabolism.

Henry L. Nadler graduated from NUMS, trained at New York University, returned to CMH in 1965, and pioneered amniocentesis for prenatal diagnosis of genetic disorders. He was appointed chair of pediatrics at NUMS and CMH chief of staff at age 34, serving from 1970 to 1981. He further expanded full-time staff and established neonatology (first led by Dr. Carl Hunt), gastroenterology (Drs. John Lloyd-Still, later, Peter Whitington and Barry Wershil), nephrology (Dr. Peter Lewy), and nuclear medicine (Dr. James Conway). Research infrastructure advances occurred during his tenure.

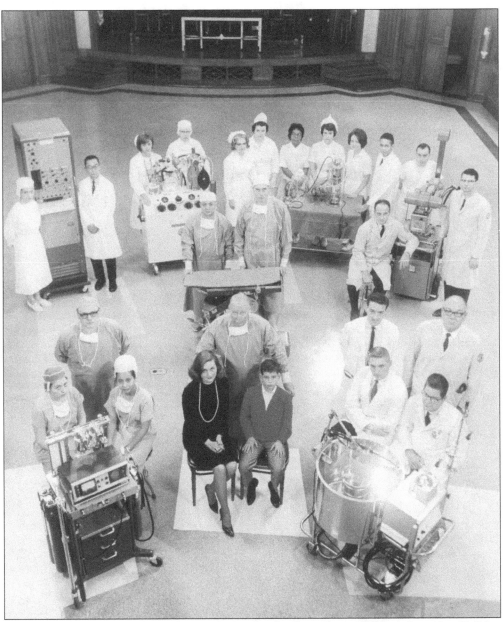

This photograph commemorates the first living unrelated renal transplant performed at CMH in February 1966, with the team involved. The 15-year-old recipient, Billy, is at center foreground with his mother. Dr. Orvar Swenson is behind Billy, with Drs. Farouk Idriss and Lowell King just behind, comprising the surgical team. In the right foreground is the dialysis team of Drs. Ahmadian and Siegel (standing); Drs. Wayne Borges (hematology) and Hugh Moffet (infectious diseases) are in the right background with many support staff. Forty years later, Billy was considered the longest US survivor of a living unrelated kidney transplant. Peritoneal dialysis at CMH was first performed in July 1961 and the first kidney biopsy in October 1961, both by Dr. Gilbert Given. The first of almost 600 pediatric kidney transplants at CMH occurred in 1964. Dr. Rick Cohn served as medical director for kidney transplantation for 20 years; Dr. Craig Langman is the current chief of kidney diseases.

CMH always excelled in pediatric education of medical students, residents, and fellows even before legendary pediatricians Drs. Brennemann and Abt in the 1920s and 1930s. Dr. Wayne Borges, who joined the hospital staff in 1963 as chief of hematology, served as director of medical education from 1971 to 1985, directing NUMS medical students, CMH residents, and postgraduate continuing education programs. He was the Given Professor in Pediatrics from 1971 to 1985.

Dr. Robert Winter (1945–1997), a graduate of Amherst who received his MD from NUMS, pediatric training at Boston Children's, and pediatric endocrinology training at Johns Hopkins, joined the CMH staff in 1975. He became CMH director of Pediatric Education in 1985, later assuming the Jacob R. Suker, MD, Chair in Medical Education at NUMS and becoming NUMS associate dean for Medical Education (1994–1997). Bob was a superb teacher and educator and was named NUMS's Teacher of the Year four times.

Dr. Harvey White's arrival in 1949 as the first full-time radiologist and chief of radiology greatly facilitated advances in clinical care and education, as demonstrated in these photographs. During his 30 years in these roles, White became a true pioneer and a national leader in the field. While reviewing an X-ray, he often stated with a twinkle, "What this child needs is a real doctor!" White recruited radiologists who were also pioneers and who developed expertise in the emerging areas of pediatric ultrasound (Dr. Arnie Shkolnik) and nuclear medicine (Dr. James Conway). Since then, interventional radiology (Dr. James Donaldson), computed tomography (CT), and magnetic resonance (MR) imaging have revolutionized imaging. Drs. Andrew Poznanski (1979–1999) and James Donaldson (1999–present) have subsequently served as chiefs of radiology (called medical imaging since 2000). Recognizable in the front row of the 1960s audience in the photograph above, taken in Bigler Auditorium, are Drs. Lawson and Borges (sitting left and center).

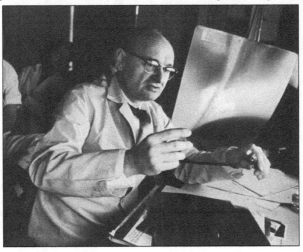

Ray and Joan Kroc, founders of McDonald's, here shake hands with movie and TV star Gary Coleman, a CMH kidney transplant recipient, at the cornerstone ceremony of the three-story Joan and Ray A. Kroc Diagnostic and Treatment Center in June 1979. This included operating rooms, radiology, emergency room, and laboratories. The addition of four floors to the existing bed tower in 1982 included an expanded Neonatal Intensive Care Unit (NICU) and a helipad.

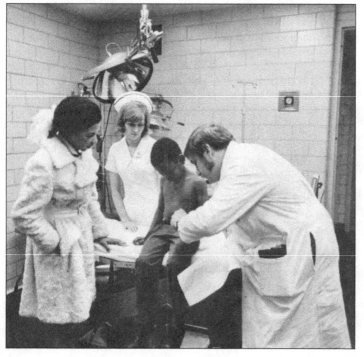

The CMH Emergency Department (ED) was designated in 1963 and located in the Wilson Building. The 1981 Kroc Center included an expanded ED, which ultimately became inadequate as visits steadily increased. In 2012, there were nearly 99,000 ED visits, an increase from 30,125 visits in 1982. Today's 45-bed Lurie Children's ED is almost double the 25-bed CMH unit. The Division of Emergency Medicine was established in 1995, with Dr. Steve Krug as the first (and current) head.

This aerial view of the CMH campus around 1982 looking west shows the campus after the 1976 construction of the parking garage on Lincoln Avenue (top left), the Kroc Diagnostic and Treatment Center (left foreground), and the additional floors of the bed tower (center). This $50 million construction was funded primarily by philanthropic support from the Kroc family, members of the Board of Directors, and many donations from grateful relatives of patients.

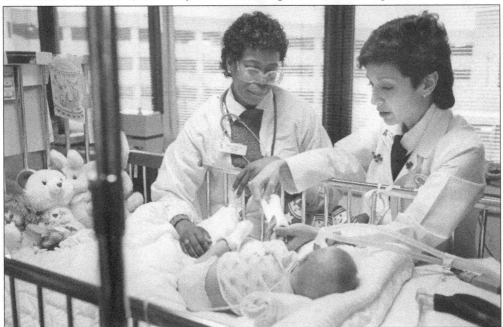

The Pediatric Intensive Care Unit (PICU) was established by the Department of Anesthesia in the 1960s with 10 beds. The Department of Pediatrics assumed leadership in 1979 under Dr. Zehava Noah, who almost single-handedly provided PICU medical care until 1990, when the Division of Critical Care was established and led by Dr. Noah until 2011. The Lefkofsky PICU now has 60 beds, with additional critical care resources in the 36-bed Regenstein Cardiac Care Unit at Lurie Children's. The new hospital was named for philanthropist and former CMH PICU nurse Ann Lurie and her late husband, Robert H. Lurie.

Dr. Mihran "Myke" Tachdjian joined the CMH staff in 1964 as chief of orthopedics (1964–1985). Educated at American University of Beirut and in orthopedics at NUMS and Boston Children's, he became world-famous in this field. He was one of three founders of the Pediatric Orthopaedic Society (1969) and authored the first internationally recognized text in this subspecialty, the 1,700-page *Pediatric Orthopaedics* (1972). He also initiated the International Pediatric Orthopaedic Symposium, which continues to be held.

After receiving his MD from University of Michigan and PhD from NUMS, Dr. David McLone joined CMH in 1975, serving as chief of neurosurgery from 1978 to 2001. He helped found and served as president of the American Society of Pediatric Neurosurgeons, was chair of the American Board of Pediatric Neurosurgery, and established and edited the journal *Pediatric Neurosurgery*. He established the Spina Bifida Clinic at CMH, one of the largest and most distinguished in the world.

Dr. Mila Pierce Rhoads (1901–1997), pictured standing in the center, a 1925 MD graduate of Rush/University of Chicago and a 1927 CMH pediatric resident, was urged by Dr. Joseph Brennemann, at left, to study pediatric blood disorders. She became a pioneer in pediatric hematology/oncology. After serving in World War II, she established pediatric hematology clinics at CMH, Rush, and the University of Chicago. At CMH, she studied leukemia with Dr. Irving Schulman, participated in early chemotherapy studies, and served on the Executive Committee of the Children's Cancer Cooperative Group. She received the initial Distinguished Career Award from the American Society for Pediatric Hematology/Oncology, was named Illinois Pediatrician of the Year, and was president of the Chicago Pediatric Society. In 1971, three children with a heavy paper bag came to CMH, seeking Dr. Pierce. They indicated they would give it only to the lady hematologist. Inside was a plastic bowl crammed with $20 in coins. "For your research," they said. Their friend, a girl whose life was lost because a cure for leukemia had not yet been found, had died recently.

Dr. Milton Paul joined CMH in 1958 as cardiologist from Boston Children's with a strong cardiac physiology research background. He served as chief of cardiology (1963–1984) and remained on staff until 1993. With Drs. Alex Muster (chief of cardiac catheterization lab, 1961–1993), Hans Wessel (director of pulmonary function and exercise lab, 1968–1996) and many others, CMH became a leader in cardiac care and research in children with cardiopulmonary disease. Dr. Barbara Deal is the current chief of cardiology.

Dr. John Raffensperger trained at Cook County Hospital and came to CMH in 1970. He was a longtime chief of pediatric surgery (1973–1996) and was CMH surgeon-in-chief (1981–1996). He edited the 1980 edition of Swenson's classic textbook *Pediatric Surgery* and was nationally recognized in his field, with many outstanding trainees, including Drs. Marleta Reynolds, later surgeon-in-chief at CMH (2009–present), and R. Lawrence Moss. Raffensperger received the Arnold M. Salzberg Mentorship Award from the American Academy of Pediatrics Section on Surgery in 1998.

Six

THE GOLDEN YEARS
1983–2012

During its last 30 years in Lincoln Park, pediatrics at CMH was led by Drs. James A. Stockman III (1984–1992), Martin Myers (1993–1998), and Tom Green (1999–2012). Surgery was headed by Drs. John Raffensperger (1981–1996), Robert Arensman (1996–2003), Constantine Mavroudis (2003–2008), and Marleta Reynolds (2009–present). Chief of staff Dr. Margaret O'Flynn (1981–1998) was succeeded by chief medical officers Drs. Edward Ogata (1998–2012) and Michael Kelleher.

In this final period, as CMH segued to Ann & Robert H. Lurie Children's Hospital of Chicago, there have been many outstanding hospital leaders in many fields, making it impossible to select only some for inclusion here. Omissions are unintentional and inevitable. Therefore, this task is left to subsequent historians to complete.

Phenomenal diagnostic and therapeutic advances occurred, including computed tomography (CT) and magnetic resonance imaging (MRI) in radiology, led by Drs. Andrew Poznanski (1979–1999) and James Donaldson (1999–2012). By 2012, the spectrum of diagnoses among CMH patients had evolved to include a wide variety of congenital defects, chronic disorders, and solid organ transplantation (kidney, heart, liver, small bowel), stem cell transplants, and various immunocompromised states. During this period, CMH became one of the major pediatric transplantation centers in the United States. In 1987, CMH was designated a Pediatric Trauma Center, and in 1992, CMH opened Westchester, the first of many satellite clinics, some with surgical facilities, to provide improved patient access. From 1986 to 2012, CMH treated 998,728 distinct patients. In 2001, CMH became the first pediatric hospital to receive the prestigious Magnet status for nursing excellence from the American Nurses Credentialing Center, with re-designation in 2005 and 2010.

In 1982, the CMH Research Institute was founded, with the Children's Memorial Research Center (now Lurie Children's Research Center) building on Halsted Street opening in 1995, with additional floors added in 2004 under the direction of Mary J.C. Hendrix, PhD, all supported by generous private philanthropy.

By 2012, the number of endowed chairs had grown to 53, representing broad philanthropic institutional support. Additional support included the Hand in Hand campaign from 1995–2000, which raised $137.5 million, followed by the Heroes for Life campaign for Ann & Robert H. Lurie Children's Hospital of Chicago, which raised $675 million, including the transformational $100 million gift by philanthropist Ann Lurie.

This iconic photograph above shows the chairs of pediatrics at NUMS/Northwestern University Feinberg School of Medicine (known as NUFSM since 2000) and chiefs of pediatrics at CMH from 1970 to the present, gathered at the 2012 opening of Lurie Children's. From left to right are Martin Myers (chair, 1993–1998), James A. Stockman III (1984–1992), Henry L. Nadler (1970–1981), and Thomas P. Green (1999–present). Their inspired leadership positioned CMH as one of the nation's top children's hospitals, by expanding research, education, advocacy, and clinical programs.

Patrick M. Magoon has served as president and chief executive officer of CMH and later Lurie Children's since 1997, some 20 years after starting as an intern. Under his leadership, NIH research funding has more than quadrupled, the number of children served has increased by 50 percent, and the financial status of the hospital has improved greatly. He led the effort to fund and build the magnificent hospital on the NUFSM downtown campus. He has also been a strong federal and state advocate for all matters of children's health, and is a past chair of the Children's Hospital Association and of the Illinois Hospital Association.

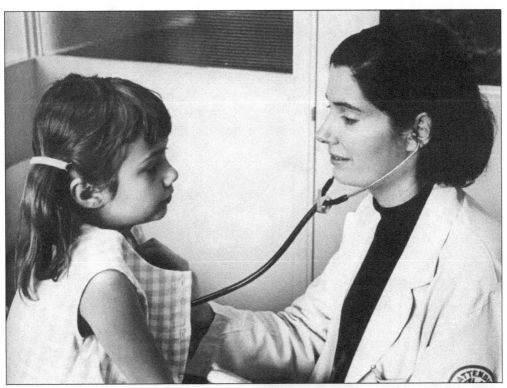

Dr. Margaret O'Flynn was educated in the United Kingdom, graduating from Oxford and Sheffield. During her metabolism/genetics fellowship at CMH she studied phenylketonuria and then joined the staff in 1963. She became director of the Cystic Fibrosis Clinic from 1967 to 1971 and director of inpatient services from 1971 to 1981. She then assumed the role of chief of staff from 1981 to 1998, utilizing her superb pediatric skills to manage the CMH department and division heads—occasionally dealing with temper tantrums and adolescent behavior!

Dr. A Todd Davis was educated at Stanford and the University of Minnesota, and served in CDC's Epidemiologic Intelligence Service (1971–1973). He joined CMH as chief of infectious diseases (ID) in 1973, training Drs. Kathryn Edwards and Ram Yogev, outstanding ID leaders, and then became chief of general academic pediatrics (1979–2000). For four decades, he was sage advisor, mentor, superb clinician, and often Teacher of the Year. He was selected the NUFSM 2011 Mentor of the Year.

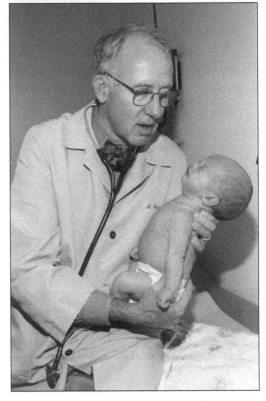

These photographs demonstrate the phenomenal growth in teaching programs at CMH over 100 years. The handful of pediatric residents of 1914 pictured above represent the earliest medical trainees at CMH. In contrast, the photograph below portrays the 2012–2013 trainees at Lurie Children's, numbering 213 residents and fellows in 33 specialties and subspecialties.

This view, looking north on Halsted Street in Lincoln Park, shows Lurie Children's Research Center. The 2004 Phase II (the Medical Research Institute Council Pavilion) added several floors of laboratories and was led by Mary J.C. Hendrix, PhD. This $25 million building and research programs tangibly represent CMH's commitment to research. The Medical Research Institute Council (now Children's Research Fund) affiliated with CMH in the early 1990s and raised substantial funds for construction of the research building.

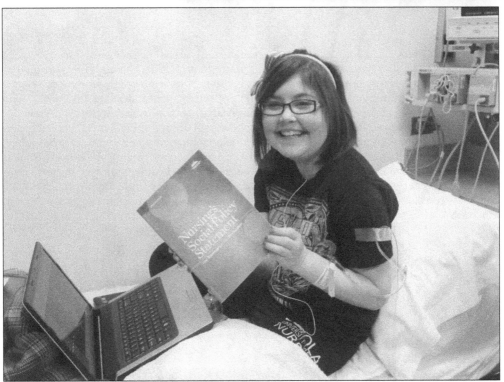

Ellen Gordon, diagnosed with juvenile rheumatoid arthritis at CMH as a child, is pictured receiving an infusion in 2011. Now a nursing student, she works part-time at Lurie Children's as a nursing assistant. Dr. Lauren Pachman, one of the world's most highly respected researchers and clinicians for pediatric autoimmune disorders and an international authority on pediatric dermatomyositis, served as chief of rheumatology 1971–2002 and continues on staff at Lurie Children's. Dr. Marisa Klein-Gitelman is the current chief of rheumatology.

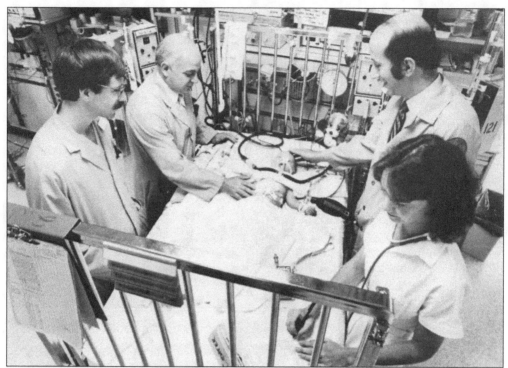

Since performing Illinois's first pediatric heart transplant in 1988, the CMH Pediatric Heart Failure and Heart Transplantation Program has become an internationally recognized resource for pediatric heart transplantation. The first child to receive a heart transplant, on May 13, 1988, was Shavell Arnold, an 18-month-old girl who survived 8.5 years with her transplant. Initiated by Dr. Farouk Idriss, second from left in the above photograph from the 1980s, and later led by Drs. Constantine Mavroudis and, then, Carl Backer, the program performed almost 200 transplants at CMH. The photograph below was taken at the first anniversary party of the heart transplant program in 1989 and includes six of the first seven transplanted patients with, from left to right, Drs. Idriss, Backer, and Zales. Shavell is the girl on her mother's lap in the front row. Dr. Elfriede Pahl has served as the medical director of the Heart Failure and Heart Transplantation Program since 1994.

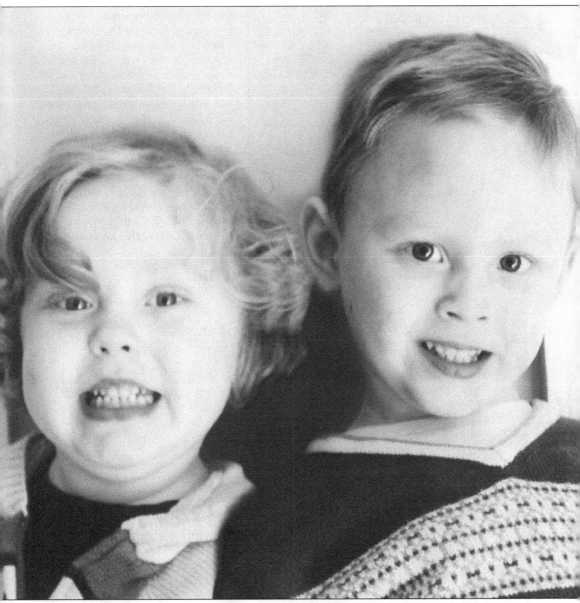

Following Children's Memorial Hospital's early success with the state's first pediatric kidney and heart transplants, the liver transplantation program was initiated in 1997 under the direction of Drs. Peter Whitington and Riccardo Superina. Among the more than 300 recipients at CMH, the Swanson twins, Jake and Luke (pictured), are believed to be the first twins in North America to have been diagnosed with biliary atresia (congenital deficiency of bile ducts) and to have undergone liver transplants. Both boys are now thriving and leading normal lives. Family members are actively involved in organ donation awareness and frequently speak at events promoting organ donation. The CMH pediatric liver transplantation program, supported by the Siragusa Transplantation Center, is the largest in the Midwest and consistently ranks as one of the 10 largest nationally. Additionally, innovative liver surgery at CMH includes the first use in North America of the novel Rex shunt surgical technique in 1997 to restore normal blood flow through the liver in children with portal hypertension.

CMH's stem cell transplant program began in 1992 under Dr. Morris Kletzel's leadership and pioneered reduced intensity transplants and use of peripheral blood stem cells. Jamarielle "Jam" Ransom-Marks was treated for leukemia at age five but relapsed, leading her to undergo a successful stem cell transplant. Jam and family became hospital spokespersons, including on the *CBS Evening News*. Since 2009, the family has held annual home blood drive/ bone marrow donor registration events. In 2012, CMH performed its 1,000th stem cell transplant.

Stephanie Flood (with her mom) is one of many patients treated in CMH's Falk Brain Tumor Center, established in 1999 by Drs. Tad Tomita (neurosurgery) and Stewart Goldman (neuro-oncology). Therapy combining surgery, radiation, and chemotherapy has been pioneered here. Stephanie, who is featured in the 2001 PBS series *Children's Hospital* shortly after successful surgery, advocates for children's hospitals and recently graduated from college.

At the age of six months, Bennett Haas became one of the youngest in the nation to receive bilateral cochlear implants for severe hearing deficit. Bennett's surgeon, Dr. Nancy Young, founder and medical director of CMH's Cochlear Implant Program, has performed 1,200 cochlear implantations since 1991. Children implanted early in life who receive intensive auditory and speech therapy are most likely to develop age-appropriate, easily understood, spoken language and literacy.

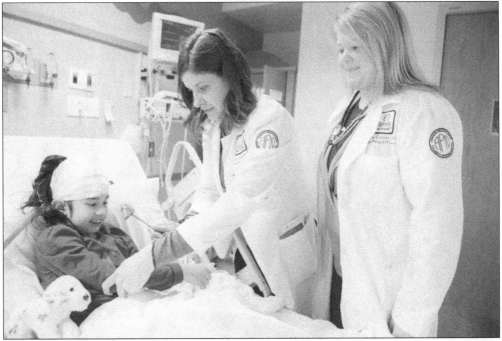

Advanced Practice Nursing (APN) has evolved over the years, with over 160 APNs assuming integral roles in most specialties at CMH, including running clinics such as the New Onset Epilepsy Clinic pictured here. In this photograph, eight-year-old Ailyn is undergoing video electroencephalogram (EEG), one of about 1,500 performed annually at the Epilepsy Center. Led by Dr. Douglas Nordli Jr., the Epilepsy Center is best known for treating children with complex and refractory epilepsy.

Dr. Stanford Shulman (right), chief of infectious diseases since 1979, greets Tomisaku Kawasaki of Tokyo on one of his three CMH visits to discuss Kawasaki disease (KD), initially described by Dr. Kawasaki. KD is the leading cause of acquired pediatric heart disease in developed countries. CMH established the Center for Kawasaki Disease in 2000 to support basic and clinical research and education related to KD. The photograph below shows, from left to right, Drs. Shulman, Ram Yogev, Anne Rowley, and Ellen Chadwick (all infectious diseases attendings) with a patient. Dr. Rowley is a world-famous researcher on etiology and pathogenesis of KD, and HIV experts Drs. Yogev and Chadwick direct the Section of Pediatric, Adolescent, and Maternal HIV Infection. These four specialists together bring over 125 years of pediatric infectious diseases experience to CMH. Dr. Yogev has garnered in excess of $50 million in extramural research grants to CMH since joining the staff in 1977.

CMH was among the earliest hospitals to develop pediatric interventional radiology (IR) in the late 1990s, with procedures including percutaneous drainage, image-guided vascular access, and needle biopsies. Over 6,000 IR procedures are performed annually, including complex ones previously unavailable for children, such as management of vascular anomalies, liver transplant patients, and techniques to support Rex shunt patients. Dr. James Donaldson, head of radiology (later medical imaging) since 1999, was the first president of Society for Pediatric Interventional Radiology.

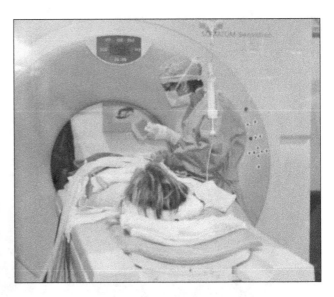

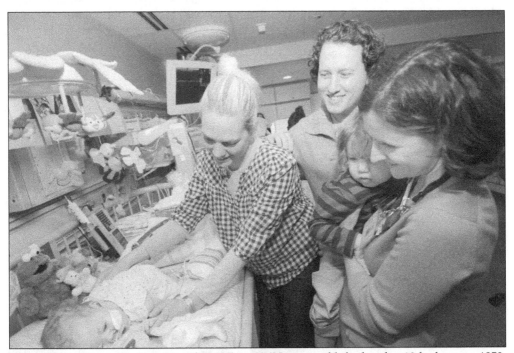

The Neonatal Intensive Care Unit (NICU) at CMH was established with a 10-bed unit in 1972. In 1974, the State of Illinois designated CMH a perinatal and neonatal center, and in 1982, a 24-bed NICU opened in the new bed tower addition. Expansion continued as neonatal care rapidly advanced technologically. Dr. Carl Hunt was the first chief of neonatology in 1975; Drs. Edward Ogata and Robin Steinhorn provided subsequent leadership.

CMH's pioneering neurosurgeon Dr. David McLone (right) presided over the March 2006 ground breaking of Illinois's first independent residence for young adults with spina bifida, Anixter Village, which opened in spring 2007. Former Chicago mayor Richard M. Daley (second from left), who lost his 33-month-old son Kevin in 1981 to spina bifida, attended along with spina bifida patient Courtney Daly.

Chicago's former first lady Maggie Daley spoke eloquently at the ground breaking for Lurie Children's on April 21, 2008, and was a longtime supporter of Children's Memorial. The Daleys established Kevin's Garden at CMH in 1993 and again at Lurie Children's in their son's memory.

Mayor Rahm Emanuel visits with Jackson Green in December 2011, maintaining the decades-long tradition of Chicago mayoral holiday visits, marking the final one at CMH. Mayor Emanuel—whose pediatrician father, Ben, long served on the CMH staff (1961–2004)—was a CMH patient at 17 for an infected traumatically amputated middle finger. At the Lurie Children's ground-breaking ceremony, he spoke movingly of his gratitude for the care he received from Drs. Ram Yogev and A Todd Davis.

CMH has initiated many programs to promote children's health beyond the hospital walls, including building safer playgrounds in underserved Chicago communities in collaboration with the Kohl's Care for Kids Safety Network. In 2012, CMH invested over $118 million in community benefit programs. Treating more children insured by Medicaid than any other hospital in the state, over 50 percent of its patients, CMH was deemed a safety-net hospital by the State of Illinois in 2012.

This view is from the roof of the CMH garage on Lincoln Avenue. The slogan "The City is Yours" is from the closing ceremony for families whose children had died at CMH, held before the hospital's move to the new downtown facility. The closing ceremonies also included a Move for the Kids walk event, covering the 3.1 miles from CMH to the new Lurie Children's.

Sarah Baine, president of the Founders' Board (originally the Board of Lady Managers in 1892), locks the doors at CMH for the last time on June 9, 2012, after all 127 patients were moved safely to Lurie Children's. On move day, Founders' Board members served as a welcoming committee for families coming to the new hospital at 225 East Chicago Avenue.

Lurie Children's ribbon-cutting ceremony on June 4, 2012, featured Ann Lurie and hospital president and chief executive officer Patrick M. Magoon (right of boy, front row), surrounded by patients, government officials, and other dignitaries. Named in recognition of Ann Lurie's $100 million gift, the state-of-the-art children's hospital was made possible through contributions from over 250,000 donors who gave more than $675 million. The week of June 4–10, 2012, saw unprecedented media coverage related to the hospital's historic move.

The 23-story Lurie Children's, the world's tallest children's hospital, opened June 9, 2012, on the campus of Northwestern University Feinberg School of Medicine. The new facility provides 288 beds, all in private rooms. One of the major benefits of the new location is adjacency to Prentice Women's Hospital, which facilitates the care of critically ill newborns. Over 20 Chicago cultural institutions helped design unique child-focused interiors. (Photograph by Nick Merrick/Hedrich Blessing.)

Visit us at
arcadiapublishing.com

CPSIA information can be obtained
at www.ICGtesting.com
Printed in the USA
LVHW07*2314230518
578235LV00020B/324/P

9 781531 668761